SOULPANCAKE

CHEW ON LIFE'S BIG QUESTIONS

RAINN WILSON

DEVON GUNDRY | GOLRIZ LUCINA | SHABNAM MOGHARABI

HYPERION
NEW YORK

WWW.SOULPANCAKE.COM

Library of Congress Cataloging-in-Publication Data

SoulPancake: *Chew on Life's Big Questions* / Rainn Wilson ... [et al.].

p. cm.

ISBN 978-1-4013-1033-2

1. Philosophy. 2. Humanities. 3. Religion. 4. Psychology. 5. Life. 6. Science. I. Wilson, Rainn, 1968- II. Title: SoulPancake.

BD31.S64 2010

100--dc22

2010011115

Hyperion books are available for special promotions, premiums, or corporate training. For details contact the HarperCollins Special Markets Department in the New York office at 212-207-7528, fax 212-207-7222, or email spsales@harpercollins.com.

Designed by Chahn Chung & Kapono Chung

FIRST EDITION

10 9 8 7 6 5 4 3 2 1

THE GOODS

WHAT IS SOULPANCAKE?

SOULPANCAKE IS A MOVEMENT TO CHEW ON LIFE'S BIG QUESTIONS. IT'S A SPACE TO TACKLE ART, PHILOSOPHY, CREATIVITY, AND SPIRITUALITY. AND ULTIMATELY, SOULPANCAKE IS ABOUT YOU—THE THINKERS, ARTISTS, POETS, AND MISFITS WHO SEEK TO STAMP OUT STIGMAS, SHAKE UP TRUTHS, AND REDEFINE WHAT IT MEANS TO BE HUMAN.

WHAT'S INSIDE?

LIFE'S BIG QUESTIONS

QUESTIONS THAT TACKLE WHAT IT MEANS TO BE HUMAN
+
MIND-BLOWING ART FROM AROUND THE WORLD
+
ODD FACTS AND QUIRKY STATS
+
QUOTES FROM A BUNCH OF SMART PEOPLE (DEAD AND ALIVE)
+
A HANDFUL OF RELATED QUESTIONS
=
YOUR BRAIN BREWING

CREATIVE CHALLENGES

UNUSUAL ACTIVITIES THAT JUMPSTART YOUR CREATIVE MOJO AND LAUNCH YOU INTO THE WORLD.

EXPLORATIONS

CREATIVE PERSPECTIVES FROM SOME OF THE WORLD'S MOST FASCINATING MINDS.

LIFE'S little LISTS

1. CONSIDER THE TOPIC.
2. WRITE A SHORT LIST.
3. ELABORATE AS NEEDED.

RE-DEFINE

A MISH-MASH OF WORDS THAT COULD USE A MAKEOVER. DIG IN. DISSECT THEM. DECIDE WHAT THEY MEAN TO YOU.

What Do I Do?

I'M BY MYSELF

IT ALL STARTS HERE. SOULPANCAKE IS ABOUT <u>YOUR</u> DEFINITION OF WHAT IT MEANS TO BE HUMAN. SO PICK A PAGE, OPEN YOUR MIND, AND LET THIS BOOK CHALLENGE YOUR OPINIONS, EMOTIONS, AND PERCEPTIONS.

I'M A PEOPLE PERSON

LAUNCH A BOOK CLUB. TEXT YOUR FRIEND A QUESTION. LOOP A STRANGER INTO A DEBATE. THIS BOOK IS A CATALYST FOR CONVERSATION. LET THE DIALOGUE BEGIN.

I'M CRAVING CONNECTIVITY

FOR A QUICK FIX, GO TO **WWW.SOULPANCAKEBOOK.COM** UNLEASH YOUR IDEAS. UPLOAD YOUR ART. AND ENGAGE WITH OTHER READERS IN THE WORLD WIDE WEBOSPHERE.

I'M ALL DONE

NO, YOU'RE NOT. PUT ON YOUR HEADPHONES AND TACKLE ONE PAGE PER SONG. ANSWER EVERY QUESTION WITH A HAIKU. REWRITE ALL YOUR LISTS IN A PACKED SUBWAY CAR. THERE'S ALWAYS MORE TO DO. GET CREATIVE, AND ENJOY THE BOOK ALL OVER AGAIN.

VII

I'M OLDER NOW (NOT NECESSARILY WISER).

LIFE HAPPENS. WHICH MEANS YOUR OPINIONS AND ANSWERS WILL EVOLVE. REVISIT THIS BOOK OFTEN—IT'S YOUR LIVING THINK TANK.

Hi.

My name is Rainn Wilson, and I am mostly an actor. But as you can see from my name handsomely embossed on the cover of this book, I am now, apparently, an author.[1]

NOTE 1

DEAR PUBLISHER: May I have a herringbone or corduroy jacket with elbow patches and a Meerschaum pipe in my jacket photo, please? Also, if I could be seated next to a Weimaraner, that would be a delightful, literary touch. Can one rent a Weimaraner? Perhaps just Photoshop one in there. OK. Thanks.

Here goes:

Right off the bat, I'm going to answer your most burning question: Why Soul*Pancake*?

Well, quite simply, because Spirit Taco was taken.

When my friends and co-creators (Devon Gundry and Joshua Homnick) and I were brainstorming possible names for a project that dealt with spirituality, creativity, and philosophy, we spent an entire day plastering note cards on the wall.

We wanted a fun, irreverent name. The intent of the movement was to "de-lamify" spirituality, and we didn't want a name that was all precious and New Age-y. I also loved the idea of involving a food item. Not only would it stick in your head and be memorable, but we knew we wanted to "cook up" something at our website, and we wanted users to "chew on" ideas and "mix up" a big pot o' ingredients. Originally, I wanted to call the site "Metaphysical Milkshake," but considering none of us, me included, really knew what "metaphysical" meant, we opted not to go with that one.

We would come up with some terrific combinations, then check to see if the domain name was taken. Our wall was littered with a host of awesome website names that we couldn't use. Names like "Spirit Stew" and "Soul Pizza" and "Transcendental Tapas."

You try it! Here's our book's first creative challenge!

STEP 1
List evocative spiritual words. (i.e. soul, spirit, heart)

STEP 2
List catchy food items. (i.e. soup, salad, chimichanga)

STEP 3
Now mix and match. (i.e. spirit chimichanga)

STEP 4
Check nameboy.com, domize.com, or domainsbot.com to see if your website name is available.

Presto! You've created your own social networking community of people interested in Life's Big Questions™! (Oh, and good luck with that.[2])

NOTE 2 If you have, in fact, found a better name than SoulPancake, please send it to us for consideration! Email us at suckitwevealreadygotaname@soulpancake.com.

Long story short, that's how we came up with SoulPancake.

Now, to answer your next question: Why would an ungainly comic actor best known for playing an intense dork of a paper salesman help create an artsy book and website about spirituality, creativity, and philosophy? Why would "Dwight" want us to "Chew on Life's Big Questions?"

Why indeed?

The other day, on the set of *The Office*, actor Ed Helms (who plays Andy) asked me about SoulPancake: "What's this SoulPancake website I've been hearing about?"

"Well, Ed," I replied. "It's a website for people interested in exploring creativity and spirituality."

"Aren't those two things pretty much mutually exclusive?" he responded. And then we immediately moved to shoot a conference room scene where Steve Carell was wearing an enormous fat suit.

I thought about what Ed said quite a lot afterward because that's *exactly* why I started SoulPancake.

I believe art and its expression are the same as faith and its expression. Science, too, for that matter. And quite frankly, everything that urges us to create, to love, to think deeply, to breathe in the moment, to be of service, to be human. They are all different expressions of some divine, creative energy that longs to radiate out and away from the trappings of closed-hearted, selfish, animal materialism.

Albert Einstein said it best:

"ALL RELIGIONS, ARTS AND SCIENCES ARE BRANCHES OF THE SAME TREE. ALL THESE ASPIRATIONS ARE DIRECTED TOWARD ENNOBLING MAN'S LIFE, LIFTING IT FROM THE SPHERE OF MERE PHYSICAL EXISTENCE AND LEADING THE INDIVIDUAL TOWARDS FREEDOM."

Before I go digging further into these ideas, I think it's best to give some context by describing my own life's path.[3]

NOTE 3
I'm about to go a bit into my "life story" here. If this makes you gag—the pretentiousness of an actor in his 40s espousing his life's story through a spiritual and artistic prism—then you may want to stop reading.

I believe that *every* one of our lives is an artistic and spiritual journey. That's the idea behind SoulPancake—that we are *all* on a creative, philosophical, and spiritual journey.

To quote Teilhard de Chardin:

"WE ARE NOT HUMAN BEINGS HAVING A SPIRITUAL EXPERIENCE, BUT SPIRITUAL BEINGS HAVING A HUMAN EXPERIENCE."

This is what unites us. But enough about you.

I was born in Seattle, Washington. The year was 1966.

I was raised in a family of Bahá'ís. What is the Bahá'í Faith, you might ask? Well, I won't tell you. Google it. Or, better yet, try reading an actual book about it. (Just skip the Wikipedia entry. Wikipedia sucks because someone can hear about, let's say, "chaos theory," then Wikipedia it, and immediately hold forth about it to all of their friends because they've remembered two or three bullet points posted at 3 a.m. by a fat pharmacist from Duluth wearing soiled pajamas.)

The important thing about my family being Bahá'í was that growing up I was exposed to lots of big ideas about philosophy, art, spirituality, and the human condition.

Don't get me wrong. My parents were dysfunctional misfits who couldn't effectively parent a sack of russet potatoes. But they were good-hearted dysfunctional misfits with eclectic and expansive ideas.

My dad was an abstract painter who wrote science fiction in his spare time and worked as a sewer truck dispatcher. (I'm not making this up. His one published novel, written in one pass on an old Smith-Corona typewriter, was called *Tentacles of Dawn*. The cover featured a naked man and woman battling a giant bat. Also, if you need sewer work done in the Seattle area, make sure to patronize "Jim Dandy Sewer," still owned by my Uncle Dougie.) Dad would paint enormous oil canvases of naked women and mythical animals while singing opera at the top of his lungs. When he wasn't painting, writing, singing, or dispatching, he would travel cross-country speaking about religion, or relax and read tomes on Sufism, mysticism, or Egyptian Gods. My pops was a bit of mad genius, albeit a kind one, with a handsome, un-ironic mustache.

Although a bit lacking in the interpersonal skills department, my parents did passionately encourage me to be an artist. They also taught me many worthwhile Bahá'í spiritual tenets. Like instilling in me the belief that all people of the world should live as one loving, united human family, regardless of race, gender, or class. And the idea that all religions are one progressively unfolding revelation that comes from the one true source of all love, the Creator. Shit like that.

Until I was 5, we lived in Central America on the Caribbean (Mosquito) Coast of Nicaragua in a swampy, malarial town called Bluefields, while my parents were doing work with the Bahá'í community there. It was a crazy mélange of customs and cultures.

Here I was, an enormously tall, enormously blond, enormously white, and enormously awkward child who spoke no Spanish, living with his off-beat bohemian parents in a large, haunted Victorian house on the Caribbean coast. We had a pet sloth and a parrot and a monkey and a dog named Heironymous Bosch. I got worms and dysentery and was stung by jellyfish. We ate shrimp and plantains and black beans every night. The cigarette boats of the drug runners would pull up to the docks, and mysterious men with huge '70s sideburns would head for the local bars. I ate boar with the Miskito Indians and, true story, ended up getting the piece with the bullet in it. I flew kites in the muddy streets with the little Nicaraguan kids and watched badly dubbed movies at the local theatre (where you could bring your dog and they served tamales).

I present this colorful tapestry because by the time I moved back to Washington State to start elementary school, I was used to being the odd duck, the misfit. This "odd-duckness" would continue into my adolescence and adult life and is a great contributing factor to the weirdos that I seem to have an affinity toward portraying as an actor. Plus, I'm also kind of a weirdo.

But back to the parents.

They were the kind of people who, when the "Watchtowers" (Jehovah's Witnesses) would stop by on a Sunday morning, would invite them in instead of shooing them away. We'd serve coffee, question them about the hidden meaning of Biblical passages, and generally freak them out.

I remember once when I was about 13, a friendly Watchtower woman pulled out a pamphlet with a picture of a lion lying next to a sheep. She said something to the effect of, "You see, in the future, the lion will lie down with the lamb."

I said something to the effect of, "Really? They are literally going to lie down together and take naps? Do you really think that's what the Bible meant? Couldn't it be a kind of metaphor about how mortal enemies will come together in friendship?"

The woman stared blankly for a moment, then pointed back to the booklet and said, "No, you can see it right here in the picture. See? The lion is going to lie down with the lamb."

Now, I don't mean to poke fun at Biblical literalists; I bet she was a very nice woman. I merely use this as an example to connect with one of the spiritual precepts that I was raised with—the "individual investigation of truth." Meaning everyone has the right—even the *obligation*—to seek the truth for him- or herself. We shouldn't take the beliefs of our parents, community, or clergyman to be our own credo unless we've checked it out for ourselves.

This is the central concept of what we're trying to do with SoulPancake: Give people a safe, fun, thought-provoking space to investigate the truth. A place to decide if they really are atheists or Lutherans or secular humanists or if that's just an inherited belief structure handed down from the outside world.

At age 20, I dropped out of college and came to a crossroads. I could either go to India with my best friend and travel the world for a year or two or I could go to The Graduate Acting Program at New York University.

I was going back and forth on this choice for several months when I had a curious spiritual epiphany. It wasn't on a mountaintop or anywhere Biblical; it was at a multiplex in Boston during the 3:30 p.m. showing of *A Chorus Line*. (Spoiler alert: It's a terrible movie, don't see it.) The whole thing is filled with singing and dancing actors talking about singing and dancing and acting. They sang about "making it" and auditioning and "sending in clowns." Stuff like that. But it still managed to touch my heart. I walked out into Boston at twilight with the snow beginning to fall and I saw everything with crystal clarity. Tears rolled down my face, and I knew I had to give acting a try. I was filled with purpose and meaning and passion and vision after watching one of the worst movies of the 1980s. True story.

ALL I SAW IN RELIGION WAS HYPOCRISY.

I arrived in New York City in 1986 and promptly dyed my hair black. It seemed like the right thing to do at the time. I think it was a basic box of Clairol midnight black, complete with the rubber gloves and the 800 number to call if something goes wrong. Something went wrong. I had forgotten about my eyebrows, which were fluffy and red. I was going for "cool and mysterious," but I looked more like a psycho-killer who had just written a violent manifesto on the walls of his cabin in blood and feces.

I also decided I needed to start smoking right away. I started with a pipe because it was different (and because my crazy Aunt Wendy smoked one). To say that I looked preposterous was the understatement of the century. I moved on to cigarettes. I chose filterless Gauloises because that's what Jean-Claude Belmondo smoked in *Breathless*. I wanted

XI

to hide the fact that I was an awkward, confused suburban Seattle boy with weird parents who just wanted everyone to like him. I was going to acting school!

I had a glorious three years there. From 9 a.m. until 11 p.m., five or six days a week I was immersed in the craft of acting, smack dab in the middle of New York City.

We did deep tongue stretches and the Alexander technique. We dove into *commedia dell'arte* and juggling. We did yoga and worked on our transatlantic, intermediate A sounds. We read about Ibsen and ran light boards for the other students' shows. We wore sweatpants, talked about the Theatre of Cruelty and swilled brackish New York deli coffee.

I CONTINUED MY CREATIVE AND SPIRITUAL JOURNEY DURING THESE PATHETIC EXPLORATIONS OF CHEMICAL ESCAPISM, DESPAIR, DEPRESSION, ADDICTION, AND A GROWING HUNGER TO FURTHER MY EGO AND MY CAREER.

We sang Cole Porter. We resonated. We loudly heaved out warm-up phrases like "Ho, Joe, bring in the boat!" We listened to Romanian directors talk about "the moment." We swam in Shakespeare for hours and hours. We sighed and cried and moaned and projected, wiggling our bodies like worms or demons. For. Three. Years.

To most of you, that may sound like a really stupid waste of time. But for me, I was in heaven. For a sensitive, artsy kid who longed to act, I was the proverbial pig in shit.

It was also around this time that I turned my back on religion. Like so many 20-something-year-olds who move to the big city, there simply was no place in my life for morality, God, prayer, or Faith. All I saw in religion was hypocrisy.

To my crowd of artist friends, belief in God or religion seemed like a throwback to a previous generation. It was quaint and obsolete, a weakness of our parents and grandparents. It was a simplistic way to moralize and to live for some superstition-filled fantasyland of heaven with God, the ultimate daddy-figure, patting you on the back and telling you that you were a good kid. Faith was a crutch for the weak. Religion was there to make you feel bad and keep you oppressed. Believers were judgmental simpletons who lived in big, square states in the center of our country and equated Jesus with gun rights and hated gays and oppressed people of color, and wanted women to stay in the kitchen. Religion's

time had come. And gone.

We had found a new religion: theatre! We did fierce plays that probed the deep recesses of the human mind and soul. We created art that could change lives in a pure and visceral way. We truly believed that if we could perform, say, *Hedda Gabler*, in just the right way to just the right audience, on just the right night, that we could change someone's heart and soul and life.

Brecht was our Buddha. Shakespeare was our Abraham. Chekhov was our Christ. Pinter was our... you get the idea.

I took all my belief in the transformative power of religion and put it into the transformative power of theatre.

I did a weekly workshop with the great director Andre Gregory. We would do "plastiques," contorting our bodies over and over again in rhythmic, isolated patterns; and then we would do Chekhov monologues and emote about our lives in a kind of raw group therapy. Gregory's philosophy is that theatre is a sacred, ancient act where art, the human body, and the experiences of our souls intersected before an audience. It was primal, like the mystical shaman/actors of our ancestors summoning the gods and reenacting the hunt through theatrical storytelling.

We were a pretentious lot.

To this day, I believe that there's nothing more affecting than sitting a few yards away from an actor who is filled with emotional truth, speaking well-written lines of great power and poetry. To witness a story unfold in front of you—a story that will never exist in exactly that same way again—to laugh and cry and breathe with living actors. I still think it's one of the most affecting artistic experiences ever. Do I still think it changes lives? Nah. But it's pretty friggin' great.

This evangelical passion for the theatre guided my life for the next decade or so. Yet somehow, my artistic passions soon morphed into a passion for my career. Like so many of us in our twenties, I became career-obsessed. I no longer cared about touching hearts with Molière; I just wanted a better agent and a TV and film career. I wanted to be adored and viewed by bigger and bigger audiences. And make a little more cash.

I never made more than $17K a year doing theatre for those 10 years in New York, so I drove a moving van to make ends meet. (Even back then, my SoulPancake colors showed. Our name? The Transcendent Moving Company. Our motto? "A man, a van, a sense of higher purpose.")

It was also during this time that I started in with the proclivities of most formerly religious artists living in big cities: sex and drugs and rock 'n' roll. And drink. Lots and lots of drink.

It's an old story. I won't go into detail here, but suffice to say, what were supposed to be good, carefree days of fun for a young actor turned south and sour rather quickly.

For a while I dated a corporate lawyer/drug dealer with a Bolivian coke connection. That was not a terribly mature relationship. I drank abundantly and every social interaction revolved around alcohol. I would "wake and bake" many mornings until, one Christmas, while living in an abandoned, rat-infested brewery in Bushwick, Brooklyn, I smoked some pot that had been laced with PCP. I almost had a seizure, and I saw the face of God appear before me (to whom I swore that I would never smoke pot again (and I haven't, FYI (ever))). And then my roommate read *Raise High the RoofBeam, Carpenters* by J.D. Salinger to me until I "came down" and stopped vomiting.

I once passed out, high, in a locked bathroom at a party filled with elite hipsters and models in a Soho loft. Nothing wakes you up faster than a bunch of angry models pounding on a door, wanting to pee or do coke. (I had to run my head under ice cold water in the sink to come to, walked out bleary-eyed, vomit-stained, wobbly, and soaking wet, and was summarily asked to leave. (Stupid models.))

There are more tales of mild debauchery that I'll save for my *E! True Hollywood Story*, but they're not important right now. What is important is that I continued my creative and spiritual journey during these pathetic explorations of chemical escapism, despair, depression, addiction, and a growing hunger to further my ego and my career. Then I came to a mighty crossroads.

I felt something missing in my life. I felt empty. Here I was, living my dream of being a working actor in New York, just like those singers and dancers in *A Chorus Line*. But theater-as-religion just wasn't cutting it for me. I had a yearning that I couldn't quite express, so I decided to re-explore this whole "God" thing.[4]

NOTE 4

Somewhere around this time I began dating my eventual wife, the beautiful and brilliant writer Holiday Reinhorn, my artistic and spiritual soul mate who was a tremendous, loving influence on my growth. She greatly encouraged me forward in this quest, and it's a journey we're taking together. She's awesome. And she's a much better writer than me.

It was also around this time that I decided to move that one very difficult step from avowed atheist to agnostic. I

started to ask my friends about God. To a person, they all had the same response: "Well, I *kinda* believe in God. I mean, I don't believe in a judgmental old man with a beard who is looking down from a cloud, scowling at us. But I *kinda* believe in a powerful, creative force out there in the stars and nature and the universe. *Kinda*."

It was all very vague.

I decided I couldn't really live as an agnostic. I had to know the answer to one of life's all-time biggest questions. I didn't want to be like so many others and have some unexplored, unexamined philosophical stance on something that was truly important. I mean, there either has to be a creator or the universe has always been as it is, beautiful and purposeless. And the fact that we are conscious and breathing and listening to *Abbey Road* and eating red velvet cake while the breeze blows in our hair is just a chance coincidence of molecules. And when we die, it's lights out, game over. That's it.

Doesn't there need to be a source to the mystery of it all? I mean, you can't *kinda* be pregnant. You either are or you aren't. It seemed to me that God was the same: There either is or there isn't a creator. It also seemed to me that one of the great mysteries of this creator in this physical world is that we're all given the choice to seek this God and to make this decision for ourselves.

> I BELIEVE ART AND ITS EXPRESSION ARE THE SAME AS FAITH AND ITS EXPRESSION.

I thought about all of this long and hard. (That's what she said.) I read books on religion and philosophy. I was reading a good deal on Native American beliefs when I stumbled upon the answer: *Wakan Tanka*.

Wakan Tanka, from what I understand, is the Lakota Sioux version of "The Great Spirit." But it is more accurately translated as "The Great Mystery." It is the animating force that inhabits the directions and nature and the sun and the earth, of which man is a part. It is love and unity, discernable, yet unknowable, running through all things.

I could get with that. The Great Mystery was not a judgmental old man with a beard sitting on a cloud.

My friend Phil and I were watching the Mets once in his apartment, talking philosophy, and I was telling him of my recent conversion to a belief in Wakan Tanka when he decided we should put it to a test. The Mets were down 5-4 at the bottom of the 9th, and he suggested we pray to Wakan Tanka.

I held up my arms in prayer in his ramshackle apartment: "Oh great spirit Wakan Tanka, who directs the winds and puts minerals in the soil and gives us plentiful food to eat. If it is your will, please allow Darryl Strawberry to hit a home run and win the game."

What I'm about to tell you may be a coincidence, but it is not an exaggeration. Promise. As soon as I finished my prayer, THWACK. Darryl Strawberry hit a two-run homer, and the Mets won. Phil and I looked at each other, jaws dropped. I don't remember what happened after that. We probably played some Bob Dylan songs on our guitars and ate whole-wheat pizza.

I also thought around this time that if there *is* a God, that surely this God must *want* something from us. Surely this God must have some kind of *plan*.

DOESN'T THERE NEED TO BE A SOURCE TO THE MYSTERY OF IT ALL? I MEAN, YOU CAN'T *KINDA* BE PREGNANT. YOU EITHER ARE OR YOU AREN'T. IT SEEMED TO ME THAT GOD WAS THE SAME: THERE EITHER IS OR THERE ISN'T A CREATOR.

Surely this divine energy, surging through every atom, didn't want either one billion Christians or one billion Muslims to burn in hellfire for all eternity. Surely faith wasn't a smorgasbord kind of thing where one person could meditate in front of a crystal and find God while another could sing songs in a church basement and find the same God. Or maybe it was.

This is when I decided to put my money where my soul was and to read the major books of the world's religions. I read the Bible and the Quran. *The Bhagavad Gita* of Hinduism and the *Dhammapada* of the Buddha. And eventually, the major books of the faith of my childhood—the Bahá'í works of *The Dawnbreakers, Gleanings from the Writings of Bahá'u'lláh, The Hidden Words*.

This introduction is not the place to share what I gleaned from those books. But suffice it to say, I made a long, circuitous trip back to faith. Faith in a time of lack of faith.

At this moment in history, there is a great movement once again toward secular humanism and against God and religion. This is completely understandable considering the hypocrisy of religion and the horrors that have been committed in its name. Religion in this day and age seems to be rote superstition seeped in dutiful dogma.

There are debates on TV, the Internet, and in books, proving or disproving God. It feels oddly like the debates that

happened a hundred years ago when Marxism and Leninism were being wrestled with around the world. The odd thing to me is that the "anti-God" coalition seems as angry, reactionary, and judgmental as the "religious" side of the debate. It's all quite funny. No one is ever going to convince anyone else to change his or her beliefs (or disbelief). Especially through "debate."

The only way I can know God, the divine, the sacred, the creator is through experience. Not intellect. I love my son. I love music. Both of those things touch my heart. No one could ever debate me and convince me that the reason they touch my heart is because of some social or physiological or behavioral wiring. I *know*. I *feel*. I *experience*.

When I hear Radiohead live, I am transported to another sphere, immeasurably and rapturously moved. When my son pops his head out of a swimming pool, his hair haloed by sunlight, and says, "Hi Dada!" my heart is touched in a profound and tangible way—as if I'd been punched in the stomach. You could lecture me for three years that all of those responses were simply chemical reactions in my brain, but it wouldn't matter. I know what I know.

I believe that we experience the divine in the same way we experience music, love, and memory. In a visceral, heart-centered way, not an intellectual one.

The hippies and the Christians used to say (with slightly different attitudes) that "God is love." That is true. God is literally love. God is also gravity. God is light and electricity. God is wind and the color green. God is chaos theory and music and that ineffable tiny sadness that we all hold in the hands of our hearts.

This makes me think back to what Ed Helms said about art and faith being mutually exclusive. It is really only in today's world that art and faith and philosophy are fractured and compartmentalized.

We live in a time where art that no one relates to is available for far too much money in galleries for millionaire collectors. Where faith is something that is methodically and dutifully expressed at specific times on Friday nights or Sunday mornings and not really considered much the rest of the week. Philosophy is something you study in college, where you learn a bunch of meaningless intellectual buzzwords that have no application to life in the real world. None of these three things ever really intersect in contemporary Western culture. They don't grab and guide us and give our lives meaning and hope.

I suppose what I've always been searching for (sometimes successfully, sometimes not) is integration and integrity. My work, my faith, my beliefs (which are separate from faith), my family, my art, and my friends all seem to inhabit different spheres, while I want them all to be a single expression of who I am, branches from the same tree.

Oftentimes, when you walk through a museum to get to the art you really want to see (or the gift shop or the restaurant), you walk past a bunch of urns and rugs and crap from old, native cultures that you don't really care to see. But the thing that gets me about those indigenous arts and crafts is how so many different facets are linked together and expressed in their creation.

For instance, you can have a pot made by some ancient, native tribe. There might be a drawing of a mountain etched on it. This might be the mountain that overlooks the tribal grounds of the person who made the pot. The mountain might be a sacred mountain where the souls of the tribe are believed to go after death. The pot is made from the clay of that same sacred mountain and was dedicated to the spirits of the mountain. The pot once held water from a river that flowed down from that mountain. That pot is beautiful and expresses something unique about the craftsman who made it.

In other words, *all* things are integrated and expressed in this fictional pot. It expresses the artist, the tribe, their history, the social web of their village, the divine. Countless things are inhabited in and radiate from this one simple, practical clay pot that hundreds of people walk by in the museum, oblivious to its meaning, every day.

But throughout mankind's history, from the ancient Greeks and Egyptians, to Rome and the Renaissance, to the glorious spiritual and artistic cultures of China and India, these seemingly divergent expressions of mankind were *not* seen as separate, but as a single, united expression of what it is to be "a spiritual being having a human experience."

I've always felt most alive and most connected when reaching for transcendence, for meaning, for the eternal. Whether that was through playing *Hamlet* or in meditation, listening to Led Zeppelin or reading the Holy Writings. Art and faith are related because they show us that there is something beyond the beyond. They give us meaning and connect us to the world behind the one that we see and taste and feel. The cloud of unknowing. They tap us into Wakan Tanka, the great mystery of life.

As Dylan Thomas said:

"THE FORCE THAT THROUGH THE GREEN FUSE
DRIVES THE FLOWER, DRIVES MY GREEN AGE,
WHICH BLASTS THE ROOTS OF TREES IS MY
DESTROYER."

And the poet Rumi said:

"THE TRUE WORK OF ART IS BUT A SHADOW OF
THE DIVINE PERFECTION."

Joseph Campbell, the philosopher of mythology, says:

"BEHIND ALL THESE MANIFESTATIONS IS THE
ONE RADIANCE, WHICH SHINES THROUGH
ALL THINGS. THE FUNCTION OF ART IS TO
REVEAL THIS RADIANCE THROUGH THE
CREATED OBJECT."

I'm really rolling with the quotes now. Here's another fave from 'Abdu'l-Bahá, the great Bahá'í teacher:

"IN THIS WONDROUS NEW AGE, ART IS
WORSHIP. THE MORE THOU STRIVEST TO
PERFECT IT, THE CLOSER WILT THOU COME TO
GOD ... WHEN THY FINGERS GRASP THE PAINT
BRUSH, IT IS AS IF THOU WERT AT PRAYER IN
THE TEMPLE."

OK, enough with the quotes. You get the idea.

Thanks for buying this book and for reading my first-ever introduction! I enjoyed writing it, and I hope I didn't come across as a pretentious douche-tard.

You'll like what's inside. Questions. Art. Thoughts. Essays. Poems. Quotes. Challenges. All designed to tickle the reader into engaging in the gooey, scary stuff of what it is to be human.

The book is fun. And cool to carry around. Or put on a handsome shelf. Or casually leave out on a coffee table as a conversation starter. Or throw like a discus at the side of the head of an attacker.

Wait! One more quote. Promise:

"I SHUT MY EYES IN ORDER TO SEE."
// PAUL GAUGUIN

That kind of sums it all up. But don't shut your eyes while driving because that would be stupid. And please don't shut your eyes while looking at this book because then you won't be able to read it. And that would also be stupid.

Rainn out. ▪

XV

LOVE, SEX &
RELATIONSHIPS

LOVE
ATTRACTION
MARRIAGE
FAMILY
COMMUNICATION
MEN & WOMEN
STRANGERS
LOSS
WHAT IS A SOUL MATE?

LIFE, DEATH &
LIVING

LEGACY
CHILDHOOD
SERVICE
ACTIVISM
FEAR OF DEATH
PRIORITIES
LIFE AFTER DEATH
PURPOSE
FEELING ALIVE
WHAT IS SUCCESS?

INTROSPECTION,
REFLECTION &
IDENTITY

SELF-IMAGE
EGO
SECRETS
MEDITATION
RIGHT & WRONG
INTUITION
FAITH
AWARENESS
TRANQUILLITY
WHAT IS PRAYER?

SCIENCE &
TECHNOLOGY

ETHICS OF TECHNOLOGY
GENETICS
ANIMALS
INVENTIONS
HEALTH
HUMAN FOOTPRINT
ENVIRONMENT
GADGETS
WHAT IS PROGRESS?

VIRTUES & VICES

HATE
GENEROSITY
GREED
DETACHMENT
SACRIFICE
GOSSIP
HUMOR
LYING
ACCOUNTABILITY
WHAT IS EVIL?

EXPERIENCES & EMOTIONS

KNOWLEDGE
MISTAKES
CHOICES
DEPRESSION
CONTROL
ANGER
COURAGE
BEAUTY
ENRICHMENT
HAPPINESS?
WHAT IS HAPPINESS?

ART & CREATIVITY

PURPOSE OF ART
POWER OF ART
ART & THE SOUL
ORIGINALITY
IMAGINATION
INSPIRATION
MUSIC
POETRY
DISCOVERING ART
WHAT IS CREATIVITY?

GOD & RELIGION

TALKING ABOUT GOD
UNITY OF RELIGION
RELIGIOUS DOCTRINE
DOUBT
NECESSITY OF RELIGION
WORSHIP
EVOLUTION & CREATIONISM
HEAVEN & HELL
TALKING TO GOD
WHAT IS GOD?

THE BRAIN & THE SOUL

TRUTH
PHILOSOPHY
FAITH & REASON
FREE WILL
POWER OF THOUGHT
CONNECTION
EXISTENCE OF THE SOUL
INFLUENCING THE SOUL
QUESTIONING
WHAT IS SPIRITUALITY?

THE BRAIN
& THE SOUL

TRUTH

PHILOSOPHY

FAITH & REASON

FREE WILL

POWER OF THOUGHT

CONNECTIONS

INFLUENCING THE SOUL

EXISTENCE OF THE SOUL

QUESTIONING

WHAT IS SPIRITUALITY?

WHERE SKIES ARE BURIED DEEP

Deep in me
there is an answer.
Deep in me
there is a cure.
Deep in me
I found a gentler self
that washed upon a shore.

And the children
slowly gathered.
None of them
had ever seen.
None of them
had dared imagine
how their lives looked
from a dream.

There's no other way
around this,
it's internal
buried deep.
Beneath
labyrinthine
thought tunnels
where the questions
pile in heaps.

Heaped upon that
is a mystery.
Heaped upon that
is a plan.
Heaped upon that
the simplicity
of a river
through the land.
And the cows
around that river
do not graze until the sea.
They are inland
bred and treasured
through their own complicity.

And the answers
are apparent.
Difference
is all the same.
I'm a whale
of deepest regions
where the ocean floor's aflame.

And the source
of this great fire
is internal
buried deep
where the blood
of stars configure
in volcanic memory.
And they push
beyond the surface.
And they push upward
and out.

From the depths
of our great sorrows
to the pucker
of a mouth:
Kiss kiss kiss
another century.
Kiss kiss kiss
another year.
Kiss kiss kiss
another species.
Kiss kiss kissed
to disappear.

And we kiss
to cross the threshold
to our present state of mind
where our feelings
fly from memories
that rest behind
the eye.

And our dreams
are deep polluted
by such tragedies
as wealth

And the fish forget
they're swimming
and their fins
morph into tails
and the truth
like evolution
is evolving
as it fails
to keep up
with the demands
of this modern space
and sea
and the skyline
of this city
are the whales
we used to be.

And I feel
these kids
around me
as I'm perched
on sandy shore
and they're touching me
and asking if I'd like
some water or if I am
already dead. So I open
up my eye and I'm staring
through an arid wind
at white whales in the sky.

And I notice
how they're floating.
And I wonder
if they see
distant cousins
in the world beneath
where skies are buried deep.

1

// **SAUL WILLIAMS,** *poet, writer, actor, artist,*
and musician

"INTENSE FEELING TOO OFTEN OBSCURES THE TRUTH." // **HARRY TRUMAN**

"OUR ABILITY TO MANUFACTURE FRAUD NOW EXCEEDS OUR ABILITY TO DETECT IT." // **VIKTOR TARANSKY**, *S1m0ne*

HOW DO YOU DETERMINE TRUTH?

3

DIG DEEPER

WHAT IS TRUTH? // DOES TRUTH EVOLVE? // WHAT'S ONE THING YOU KNOW FOR SURE?

A STUDY BY THE PEW INTERNET & AMERICAN LIFE PROJECT REVEALS THAT ONLY 25% OF THOSE WHO SEARCH THE INTERNET FOR HEALTH TOPICS CHECK THE SOURCE AND DATE OF THE INFORMATION REGULARLY TO ASSESS ITS QUALITY.

SOURCE: DOES IT REALLY MATTER?

COPERNICUS WAS THE FIRST TO SUGGEST THAT THE EARTH AND PLANETS REVOLVE AROUND THE SUN—A THEORY SUPPORTED BY GALILEO, JOHANNES KEPLER, AND ISAAC NEWTON. COPERNICUS, HOWEVER, DELAYED PUBLISHING HIS FINDINGS SO AS NOT TO INCUR THE WRATH OF THE CATHOLIC CHURCH, UNLIKE GALILEO, WHOSE CHAMPIONING OF THE HELIOCENTRIC VIEW OF THE UNIVERSE LED TO HIM BEING DENOUNCED DURING THE ROMAN INQUISITION.

SOURCE: "GALILEO'S RELIGION" BY OLAF PEDERSEN, FROM *The Galileo Affair: A Meeting of Faith and Science* **(VATICAN OBSERVATORY, 1985)**

SIDEWALK

"IT IS UNBECOMING FOR YOUNG MEN TO UTTER MAXIMS." // ARISTOTLE

WE DARE TO DISAGREE WITH ARISTOTLE—AGE ISN'T THE ONLY PREREQUISITE FOR WISDOM. SO LET'S CHALLENGE THIS OLD GREEK BRAINIAC, AND PROCLAIM OUR PHILOSOPHIES TO THE WORLD.

STEP 1

SUM UP YOUR PERSONAL PHILOSOPHY ON LIFE.

STEP 2

HIT UP A 6-YEAR-OLD FOR SOME CHALK. OR GO BUY SOME, CHEAPSKATE.

SCRIBE

STEP 3

FIND PAVEMENT.

STEP 4

BUST OUT YOUR PSEUDO-INNER-VANDAL AND SCRAWL YOUR MESSAGE FOR THE WORLD TO SEE

5

How do you reconcile discrepancies between reason and faith?

6

DIG DEEPER

WHEN HAS REASON FAILED YOU?
WHAT DO YOU BELIEVE STRICTLY ON FAITH?
DOES EVERY QUESTION HAVE AN ANSWER?

"THE WAY TO SEE BY FAITH IS TO SHUT THE EYE OF REASON." // **BENJAMIN FRANKLIN**

SOME OF HISTORY'S GREATEST SCIENTISTS—
GALILEO GALILEI, ISAAC NEWTON, RENÉ DESCARTES,
ROBERT BOYLE, AND GREGOR MENDEL—WERE
DEVOUT BELIEVERS IN GOD.

A SOLID MAJORITY OF AMERICANS (61%) SAY THAT
SCIENCE DOES NOT CONFLICT WITH THEIR OWN
RELIGIOUS BELIEFS.
SOURCE: THE PEW RESEARCH CENTER

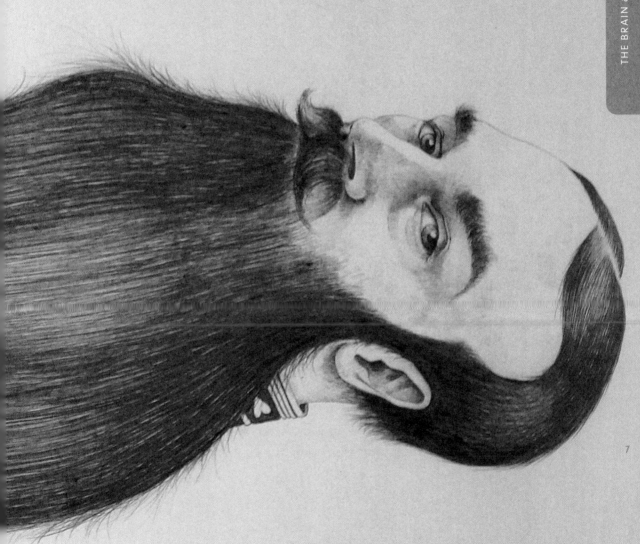

7

"BOTH FAITH AND REASON DISCOVER TRUTH, A CONFLICT BETWEEN THEM BEING
IMPOSSIBLE SINCE THEY BOTH ORIGINATE IN GOD." // **ST. THOMAS AQUINAS**

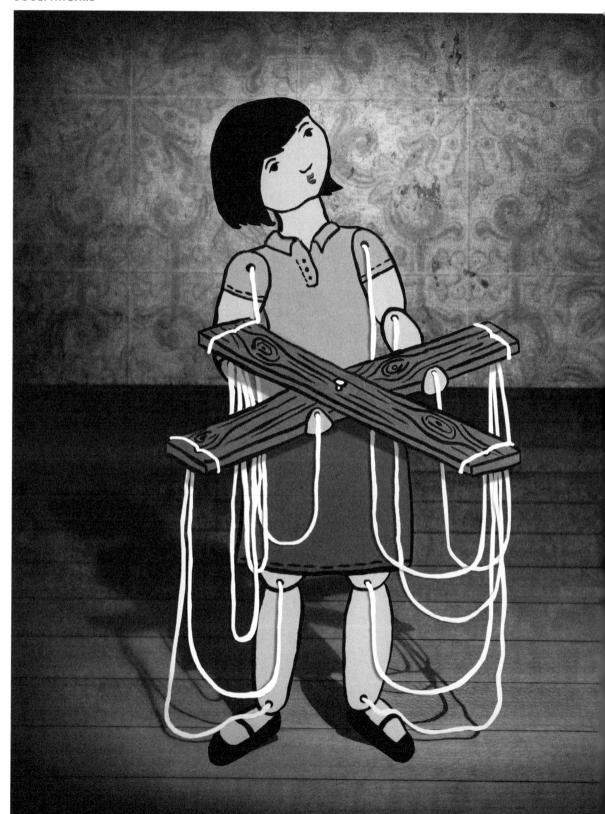

8

THE WORD **"FATE"** IS NOT MENTIONED ANYWHERE IN THE KING JAMES BIBLE.

THE MONTH YOU ARE BORN CAN PREDICT HOW GOOD, OR BAD, A DRIVER YOU ARE. LIBRAS ARE THE WORST DRIVERS AND CAUSE THE MOST ACCIDENTS; LEOS ARE THE SAFEST.

SOURCE: INSURANCEHOTLINE.COM

WHAT IS THE INTERPLAY BETWEEN
FATE AND FREE WILL?

9

 DIG DEEPER

IS IT POSSIBLE TO INFLUENCE THE FATE OF OTHERS? WHEN HAVE YOU FELT LIKE YOU HAD NO FREE WILL? WHAT IS THE COLLECTIVE DESTINY OF HUMANITY?

"MAN IS A BEING WITH FREE WILL; THEREFORE, EACH MAN IS POTENTIALLY GOOD OR EVIL, AND IT'S UP TO HIM AND ONLY HIM (THROUGH HIS REASONING MIND) TO DECIDE WHICH HE WANTS TO BE." // **AYN RAND**

"YOU CAN'T INTERFERE WITH DESTINY, THAT'S WHY IT'S DESTINY. IF YOU TRY TO INTERFERE, THE SAME THING IS GOING TO HAPPEN ANYWAY AND YOU'LL JUST SUFFER." // **TRACY FLICK,** *Election*

"ONCE YOU MAKE A DECISION, THE UNIVERSE CONSPIRES TO MAKE IT HAPPEN."
// **RALPH WALDO EMERSON**

"YOU CAN DREAM, CREATE, DESIGN, AND BUILD THE MOST WONDERFUL PLACE IN THE WORLD, BUT IT REQUIRES PEOPLE TO MAKE THE DREAM A REALITY." // **WALT DISNEY**

HOW DO THOUGHTS AFFECT REALITY?

DIG DEEPER

HOW DOES PRAYER AFFECT REALITY?
WHEN HAS YOUR MIND BEEN YOUR WORST ENEMY?
HOW DO YOU KEEP CYNICISM IN CHECK?

RESEARCHERS AT THE CLEVELAND CLINIC FOUNDATION DISCOVERED THAT A MUSCLE CAN BE STRENGTHENED JUST BY THINKING ABOUT EXERCISING IT.

SOURCE: THE FRANKLIN INSTITUTE

SINCE ITS RELEASE, *The Secret* HAS SOLD 4.2 MILLION COPIES IN THE UNITED STATES ALONE AND HAS SPENT MORE THAN 150 WEEKS ON THE *New York Times* BEST SELLERS LIST.

SOURCE: *New York Times* BEST SELLERS LIST, NIELSEN BOOKSCAN

PLAYLIST FOR PEOPLE·WATCHING

LIFE CAN BE AN INTENSE, CHAOTIC, AND CONFUSING EXPERIENCE THAT WE RACE THROUGH WITH BLINDERS ON. LET'S PAUSE FOR A MOMENT AND TAKE IT ALL IN.

"WHEN WE GET TOO CAUGHT UP IN THE BUSYNESS OF THE WORLD, WE LOSE CONNECTION WITH ONE ANOTHER—AND OURSELVES."

// JACK KORNFIELD

STEP 1. GO TO A CROWDED PUBLIC PLACE.

STEP 2. PUT ON YOUR HEADPHONES. HIT "PLAY."

STEP 3. SIT BACK. WATCH THE WORLD—AND THE SOULS YOU SHARE IT WITH—GO BY.

13

ACCORDING TO A RECENT SURVEY OF THE AUTHORS OF THIS BOOK, **SOULPANCAKE.COM** IS THE NO. 1 PLACE ON THE INTERNET TO REFUEL YOUR SOUL.

TALK ABOUT HIGHER LEARNING. A NATIONAL STUDY OF COLLEGE STUDENTS FOUND THAT, BETWEEN THEIR FRESHMAN AND JUNIOR YEARS, ATTENDANCE OF RELIGIOUS SERVICES DECREASED WHILE OVERALL LEVELS OF SPIRITUALITY—A SEARCH FOR MEANING, PURPOSE, AND SELF-UNDERSTANDING—INCREASED.

SOURCE: THE PEW FORUM ON RELIGION & PUBLIC LIFE

WHAT DRAINS YOUR SOUL?
WHAT RECHARGES IT?

 DIG DEEPER

WHAT IS THE SOUL?
CAN YOU KILL YOUR SOUL?
DOES THE SOUL HAVE A GENDER?

"MUSIC WASHES AWAY FROM THE SOUL THE DUST OF EVERYDAY LIFE."
// BERTHOLD AUERBACH

"THE USE OF THE ATOMIC BOMB, WITH ITS INDISCRIMINATE KILLING OF WOMEN AND CHILDREN, REVOLTS MY SOUL."
// HERBERT HOOVER

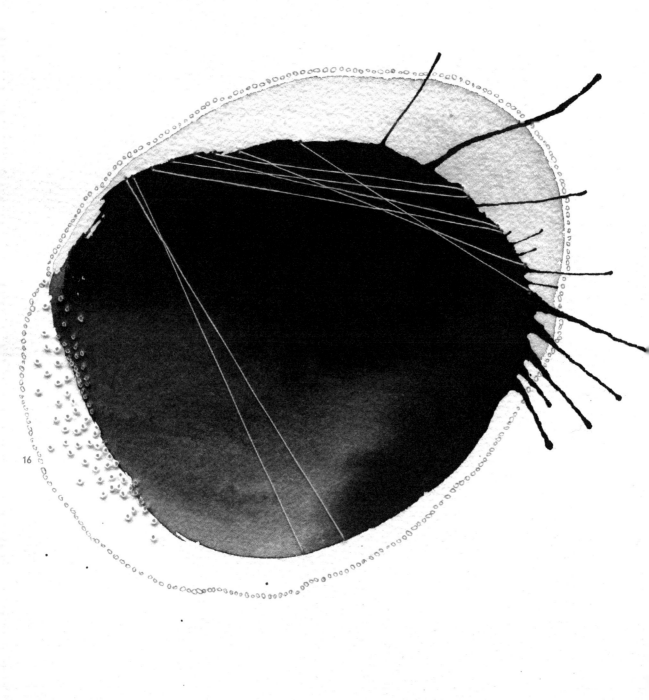

SOUL SCRIBBLE

VISUALIZE YOUR SOUL FOR A MOMENT. NOW SCRIBBLE, SKETCH, OR RIP UP THOSE OLD MAGAZINES YOU HAVE LYING AROUND, AND CREATE YOUR TAKE ON WHAT YOUR SOUL "LOOKS" LIKE BELOW.

"IF YOU NEED TO VISUALIZE THE SOUL, THINK OF IT AS A CROSS BETWEEN A WOLF HOWL, A PHOTON, AND A DRIBBLE OF DARK MOLASSES. BUT WHAT IT REALLY IS, AS NEAR AS I CAN TELL, IS A PACKET OF INFORMATION. IT'S A PROGRAM, A PIECE OF HYPERSPATIAL SOFTWARE DESIGNED EXPLICITLY TO INTERFACE WITH THE MYSTERY." // **TOM ROBBINS**

TELL ME NOW!

LIST FIVE QUESTIONS YOU *HATE* NOT HAVING THE ANSWERS TO.

1.

2.

3.

4.

5.

SPIRITUALITY

SPIR·IT·U·AL·I·TY | spiri CH ōō'alitē | noun

1. of, relating to, consisting of, or affecting the spirit; incorporeal
2. **a)** of or relating to sacred matters
   b) ecclesiastical rather than lay or temporal
3. concerned with religious values
4. related or joined in spirit
5. **a)** of or relating to supernatural beings or phenomena
   b) of, relating to, or involving spiritualism

SYNONYMS
INCORPOREALITY, OTHERWORLDLINESS, UNEARTHLINESS, DEVOUTNESS, HOLINESS, PIOUSNESS, RELIGIOSITY, RELIGIOUSNESS

"I WOULD DESCRIBE MY SPIRITUALITY AS EXACTLY THE OPPOSITE OF HAVING A RELIGIOUS AFFILIATION." // BILL MAHER

"OUR GENERATION HAS HAD NO GREAT WAR, NO GREAT DEPRESSION.

OUR WAR IS SPIRITUAL.

OUR DEPRESSION IS OUR LIVES."
// CHUCK PALAHNIUK

"A LIFE IS EITHER ALL SPIRITUAL OR NOT SPIRITUAL AT ALL. NO MAN CAN SERVE TWO MASTERS. YOUR LIFE IS SHAPED BY THE END YOU LIVE FOR. YOU ARE MADE IN THE IMAGE OF WHAT YOU DESIRE."
// THOMAS MERTON

"Spirituality can be severed from both vicious sectarianism and thoughtless banalities. Spirituality, I have come to see, is nothing less than the thoughtful love of life."

// ROBERT C. SOLOMON

"The first act of awe, when man was struck with the beauty or wonder of nature, was the first spiritual experience." // HENRYK SKOLIMOWSKI

20

YOU RE-DEFINE

SPIRITUALITY IS

SPIRITUALITY ISN'T

ART & CREATIVITY

11 THINGS THAT FUEL MY CREATIVITY

1. Making lists.

2. Being attuned to the divine or mystical winds—so long as those winds are carrying marijuana smoke.

3. Friction between my economical base and my desire to purchase marijuana.

4. Deadlines.

5. The combination of a fist full of googly eyes and an object without them.

6. Toadstools, woodland creatures, and miniature furniture—because I find them magical.

7. Other people's drama, including skin disorders and flat tires.

8. The understanding that because the things that interest me are usually unique to me, I'm forced to generate my own projects.

9. Playing, in the way children do—completely uninhibited, with the singular goal of making the other laugh.

10. Costumes, wigs, and theatrical sets.

11. Making faces.

11 THINGS THAT DRAIN MY CREATIVITY

1. Calling myself a creative person.

2. Electronic noise—a television, a radio, phones ringing. Cellular phones in general, actually. I don't like cellular phones. I don't like the way they look or sound. I don't like to be in the same room with one, whether someone is talking on it or not.

3. Having to repeat myself. This one is important, so I'll say it again. Twice. Having to repeat myself. Having to repeat myself. I need to lie down.

4. Deadlines.

5. Having to make changes in order to please someone else.

6. Reading a screenplay, classical music, and brunch. I list these together because not only do they not inspire my creativity, they make me sleepy.

7. Rug shopping. I don't know if it's the smell, the creepy salesmen, or trying to figure out dimensions.

8. Airports.

9. Cooking for vegans.

10. Movies with big ships in them.

11. Waiting.

// **AMY SEDARIS,** *film and television actress; comedian; and author of* Simple Times

23

> "ART IS THE ACT OF TRIGGERING DEEP MEMORIES, OF WHAT IT MEANS TO BE FULLY HUMAN." // **DAVID WHYTE**

> "WHENEVER SOCIETY GETS TOO STIFLING AND THE RULES GET TOO COMPLEX, THERE'S SOME SORT OF MUSICAL EXPLOSION." // **SLASH**

Piss Christ IS A 1987 PHOTOGRAPH BY ANDRES SERRANO THAT DEPICTS A SMALL PLASTIC CRUCIFIX SUBMERGED IN A GLASS OF THE ARTIST'S URINE. IT WON AN AWARD FROM THE SOUTHEASTERN CENTER FOR CONTEMPORARY ART, WHICH WAS SPONSORED IN PART BY THE NATIONAL ENDOWMENT FOR THE ARTS, LEADING TO A DEBATE IN THE UNITED STATES SENATE ABOUT PUBLIC FUNDING OF ART.

SOURCE: *Albion Monitor*

VINCENT VAN GOGH ONLY SOLD ONE PAINTING DURING HIS LIFETIME FOR A MEASLY 400 FRANCS (ABOUT $90 TODAY). IN 1990, HIS *Portrait of Dr. Gachet* SOLD AT A CHRISTIE'S AUCTION FOR $134.6 MILLION (ADJUSTED FOR INFLATION), MAKING IT THE FOURTH MOST EXPENSIVE PAINTING EVER SOLD. THE NO. 1 SPOT BELONGS TO JACKSON POLLOCK'S *No. 5, 1948*, WHICH SOLD AT SOTHEBY'S IN 2006 FOR $148.1 MILLION (ADJUSTED FOR INFLATION).

SOURCE: *New York Times*

WHAT IS THE PURPOSE OF ART?

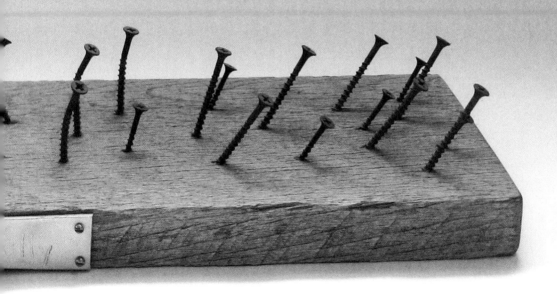

25

WHAT IS ART?

WHAT PIECE OF ART MOST SPEAKS TO YOU?

HOW DOES KNOWING THE INTENTION BEHIND A WORK OF ART AFFECT YOUR EXPERIENCE OF IT?

LIST FIVE PIECES OF ART THAT STIMULATE YOUR BRAIN STEM.

1.

DESCRIBE THE FEELING

2.

DESCRIBE THE FEELING

3.

DESCRIBE THE FEELING

4.

DESCRIBE THE FEELING

26

5.

DESCRIBE THE FEELING

ARTGASM (N.): THE OVERWHELMING AND HYPER-ORGASMIC EXPERIENCE OF VIEWING, PONDERING, OR DISCUSSING A TRULY FABULOUS PIECE OF ART.

SOURCE: URBAN DICTIONARY

IS ARTISTIC ABILITY LEARNED OR INHERENT?

WHAT ARTIST IS YOUR CREATIVE TWIN?

IS THERE A CONNECTION BETWEEN GOD AND CREATIVITY?

28

T'ai Chi TRANSLATES LITERALLY INTO THE "SUPREME ULTIMATE LIFE FORCE" AND IS A CHINESE MARTIAL ART FORM TYPICALLY PRACTICED FOR ITS HEALTH AND SPIRITUAL BENEFITS. IT IS ESTIMATED THAT MORE THAN 100 MILLION PEOPLE PRACTICE *T'ai Chi* IN CHINA DAILY TO MAXIMIZE THEIR INNER PEACE.

SOURCE: *Thirteen Treatises on T'ai Chi Ch'uan* **BY CHENG MAN** CH'ING (NORTH ATLANTIC BOOKS, 1993)

"ART IS MEANT TO DISTURB."
// GEORGES BRAQUE

"THERE IS NOTHING THAT MAKES
ITS WAY MORE DIRECTLY INTO
THE SOUL THAN BEAUTY."
// JOSEPH ADDISON

WHAT DOES ART HAVE TO DO WITH THE SOUL?

29

IN EGYPTIAN HIEROGLYPHICS, THE *"Ka,"* A U-SHAPED
SYMBOL WITH POINTED RAM'S HORNS AT THE TIPS,
USUALLY TRANSLATED INTO "SOUL" OR "SPIRIT." IT WAS
BELIEVED THAT THE RAM-HEADED GOD KHNUM CRAFTED
THE *Ka* ON HIS POTTER'S WHEEL AT A PERSON'S BIRTH.

THE WORD "PLAGIARISM" IS FROM THE LATIN *Plagiarius,* WHICH TRANSLATES TO "KIDNAPPER."

"ORIGINALITY IS UNDETECTED PLAGIARISM."
// W. R. INGE

WHERE'S THE LINE BETWEEN INSPIRATION & IMITATION?

DIG DEEPER

WHERE DO YOU FIND INSPIRATION?

IS AN IDEA EVER REALLY ORIGINAL?

DOES THE DRIVE TO BE ORIGINAL STIFLE OR MOTIVATE YOU?

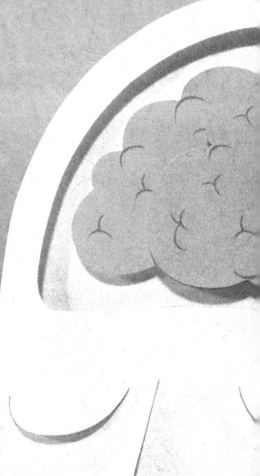

THE "AMEN BREAK" WAS A BRIEF 1969 DRUM SOLO PERFORMED BY GREGORY SYLVESTER "G. C." COLEMAN IN THE WINSTONS' SONG "AMEN, BROTHER." FREQUENTLY USED IN HIP-HOP, JUNGLE, BREAKCORE, AND DRUM AND BASS MUSIC, IT HAS BEEN CALLED "A SIX-SECOND CLIP THAT SPAWNED SEVERAL ENTIRE SUBCULTURES."

SOURCE: *Can I Get An Amen?* **BY NATE HARRISON**

"THE BEES PILLAGE THE FLOWERS HERE AND THERE, BUT THEY MAKE HONEY OF THEM, WHICH IS ALL THEIR OWN; IT IS NO LONGER THYME OR MARJORAM; SO THE PIECES BORROWED FROM OTHERS, HE WILL TRANSFORM AND MIX UP INTO A WORK ALL HIS OWN." // **MICHEL EYQUEM DE MONTAIGNE**

31

ART AT ARM'S REACH

Some artists don't have to look far to find the materials they need to create masterpieces. Now you can be one of them.

STEP 1

Scavenge around your desk, barstool, couch cushions for anything handy. And we mean anything: paper clips, poker chips, fake eyelashes, junk mail, bullet casings.

STEP 2

Create art.

STEP 3

Bask in your artistic brilliance. Repeat as desired.

> "ART ARISES WHEN THE SECRET VISION OF THE ARTIST AND THE MANIFESTATION OF NATURE AGREE TO FIND NEW SHAPES."
> // **KAHLIL GIBRAN**

PUNK-ROCK PROM DATE

DIG
DEEPER

WHY DO WE FEEL THE NEED TO CREATE?

IS A LITTLE BIT OF INSANITY ESSENTIAL FOR CREATIVE GENIUS?

HOW DOES YOUR MOOD AFFECT YOUR CREATIVE OUTPUT?

A RESEARCH STUDY FOUND THAT STUDENTS WHO EXPERIENCED LAUGHTER-INDUCING HUMOR PRIOR TO TAKING A CREATIVITY TEST PERFORMED TWICE AS WELL AS STUDENTS WHO DIDN'T. TRANSLATION: WATCH *The Office* BEFORE DOING YOUR HOMEWORK.

SOURCE: *Journal of Educational Psychology*

"IN ITALY, FOR 30 YEARS UNDER THE BORGIAS THEY HAD WARFARE, TERROR, MURDER, BLOODSHED, BUT THEY PRODUCED MICHELANGELO, LEONARDO DA VINCI, AND THE RENAISSANCE. IN SWITZERLAND, THEY HAD BROTHERLY LOVE. THEY HAD 500 YEARS OF DEMOCRACY AND PEACE, AND WHAT DID THAT PRODUCE? THE CUCKOO CLOCK."
// **ORSON WELLES**

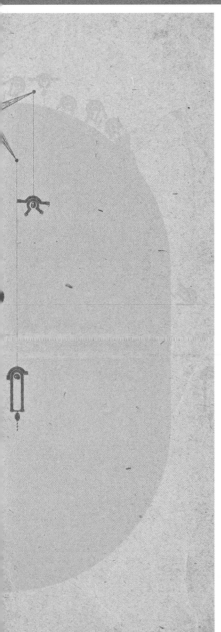

WHAT PARALYZES YOUR CREATIVITY? WHAT FUELS IT?

A PSYCHOLOGY STUDY DEMONSTRATED THAT RED PROMOTES CAUTIOUS MOTIVATION, WHICH IS CONDUCIVE TO TASKS THAT REQUIRE ATTENTION TO DETAIL.

BY CONTRAST, BLUE PROMOTES AN EXPLORATORY MOTIVATIONAL STATE, WHICH IS CONDUCIVE TO CREATIVITY.

SOURCE: *Science*

"THE LIFE OF THE CREATIVE MAN IS LED, DIRECTED, AND CONTROLLED BY BOREDOM. AVOIDING BOREDOM IS ONE OF OUR MOST IMPORTANT PURPOSES." // **SAUL STEINBERG**

MOVE OVER, TOP 40. LISTENING TO MOZART CAN, IN FACT, MAKE YOU SMARTER. THE "MOZART EFFECT" IS DEFINED AS THE "SLIGHT AND TRANSIENT IMPROVEMENT IN [SPATIAL] REASONING SKILLS DETECTED IN NORMAL SUBJECTS AS A RESULT OF EXPOSURE TO THE MUSIC OF MOZART, SPECIFICALLY HIS SONATA FOR TWO PIANOS."

SOURCE: *Companion to Clinical Neurology* **BY WILLIAM PRYSE-PHILLIPS (OXFORD UNIVERSITY PRESS, 2003)**

WHY IS MUSIC SO POWERFUL?

DIG DEEPER

WHEN HAS MUSIC MOST MOVED YOUR SOUL?

WHAT ONE SONG OR PIECE OF MUSIC SHOULD EVERY PERSON EXPERIENCE?

WHAT'S MORE POWERFUL IN A SONG— THE MUSIC OR THE LYRICS?

"MUSIC IS THE ONLY THING THAT MAKES SENSE ANYMORE. PLAY IT LOUD ENOUGH AND IT KEEPS THE DEMONS AT BAY."
// **JO-JO,** *Across the Universe*

THE WORLD'S OLDEST MUSICAL INSTRUMENTS—FLUTES MADE OF BONE AND IVORY THAT ARE AT LEAST 35,000 YEARS OLD—WERE DISCOVERED BY ARCHAEOLOGISTS IN SOUTHWEST GERMANY. ALONG WITH FOOD AND SHELTER, IT SEEMS THAT MUSIC HAS ALWAYS BEEN A BASIC HUMAN NEED.

SOURCE: *Boston Globe*

"BEAUTIFUL MUSIC IS THE ART OF THE PROPHETS THAT CAN CALM THE AGITATIONS OF THE SOUL; IT IS ONE OF THE MOST MAGNIFICENT AND DELIGHTFUL PRESENTS GOD HAS GIVEN US." // **MARTIN LUTHER**

BLACKOUT POET

"EVERY BLOCK OF STONE HAS A STATUE INSIDE IT, AND IT IS THE TASK OF THE SCULPTOR TO DISCOVER IT." // **MICHELANGELO**

Michelangelo believed that the statue was waiting in the stone—it was the sculptor's job to chip away the parts that didn't belong. Maybe the same is true about poetry. If you look long enough at a sheet of words, you can find rhythms, patterns, brilliance. The reward? The poem within. It was waiting there for you all along.

STEP 1

Grab a marker. A black one. Don't sniff it.

STEP 2

Find a single sheet of newspaper or tear a page from your favorite magazine. Even a book you wish you'd never read.

STEP 3

Black out what doesn't belong. Chisel away a word at a time until you reveal your poetic masterpiece.

the
mischief-maker
gods
were ordinary people
too
loved and
afraid
some
hid in names or
war or
the sky.

ART ATTACK!

THE CREATION AND CONSUMPTION OF ART CAN BE EXTREMELY PROFOUND AND PERSONAL EXPERIENCES. HERE ARE 52 WAYS TO JUMP IN. TRY ONE A WEEK, AND YOU'RE COVERED FOR A YEAR.

- WATCH A MUSIC VIDEO ON "MUTE."
- INSPECT THE ART ON A DOLLAR BILL.
- LOOK INSIDE A GRAND PIANO.
- LISTEN TO NO. 1 HITS FROM YOUR YEAR OF BIRTH.
- STARE AT THE PATTERNS AT A FABRIC STORE.
- EXPLORE THE PAINT SWATCHES AT A HARDWARE STORE.
- WATCH A MAKEUP ARTIST AT WORK.
- GO TO A BOOKSTORE. DON'T OPEN A SINGLE BOOK. JUST STARE AT THE COVERS.
- WATCH A PASTRY CHEF DECORATE A CAKE.
- ANALYZE A BLUEPRINT.
- GO TO AN AUCTION. CLOSE YOUR EYES. LISTEN TO THE AUCTIONEER.
- PICK UP YOUR LOCAL NEWSPAPER. ONLY LOOK AT THE PHOTOS.
- ADMIRE AN OLD BUILDING.
- LOOK AT A COMIC BOOK.
- GO TO A SLAM POETRY READING.
- EXAMINE THE BEAMS AND BOLTS OF A ROLLER COASTER.
- CLOSELY ADMIRE YOUR FINGERPRINTS.
- TAKE A GOURMET COOKING CLASS.
- WATCH A BREAKDANCER HEADSPIN.
- PUT ON A FOREIGN FILM. TURN OFF THE SUBTITLES.
- OBSERVE A FLORIST AT WORK.
- WATCH A SUSHI CHEF PREPARE NIGIRI.
- ATTEND A STUDENT ART SHOW.
- GO TO AN ART GALLERY AND ASK THE CURATOR FOR A GUIDED TOUR.
- PULL A WEED OUT OF THE DIRT AND STUDY ITS ROOTS.

- SPY ON A POODLE GETTING GROOMED.
- OBSERVE A CLASS AT A DOJO.
- LOOK UNDER THE HOOD OF A CAR.
- GO TO A HARLEY DAVIDSON STORE.
- CHECK OUT A CAREFULLY MANICURED GARDEN.
- EXAMINE THE UNDERSIDE OF A LARGE BRIDGE.
- WATCH PLANES TAKE OFF AT THE AIRPORT.
- SCRUTINIZE A SPIDERWEB.
- LOOK AT STORE SIGNS AT NIGHT.
- GO TO A YOGA STUDIO.
- SCAN THE ARRAY OF BOTTLES IN THE SHAMPOO AISLE AT THE STORE.
- HUNT FOR STREET ART IN YOUR CITY.
- GO TO A COSTUME STORE.
- TREK TO THE PLANETARIUM.
- FIND THE MOST INTERESTING WINDOW DISPLAY IN YOUR TOWN.
- WATCH A BARTENDER MIX DRINKS.
- EXPERIMENT WITH ALL THE FONTS ON YOUR COMPUTER.
- GET A PEDICURE. YES, GUYS TOO.
- GOOGLE "HEART SURGERY VIDEOS."
- ATTEND AN OUTDOOR MUSIC FESTIVAL.
- ASK A BEEKEEPER TO LET YOU OBSERVE HONEYBEES AT WORK. DON'T GET STUNG.
- WATCH A SILENT FILM.
- LOOK AT A STAINED-GLASS WINDOW.
- LISTEN TO A BEATBOXER.
- ASK TO WATCH A JEWELER SET A DIAMOND.
- TAKE A SALSA DANCE LESSON.
- OBSERVE A TATTOO ARTIST AT WORK.

CREATIVITY

THEY DEFINE

CRE·A·TIV·I·TY | krē-ā'tivitē | noun

1. marked by the ability or power to create; given to creating
2. having the quality of something created rather than imitated: imaginative
3. managed so as to get around legal or conventional limits; also, deceptively arranged so as to conceal or defraud

SYNONYMS
CLEVERNESS, GENIUS, IMAGINATION, IMAGINATIVENESS, INGENUITY, INSPIRATION, INVENTIVENESS, ORIGINALITY, RESOURCEFULNESS, TALENT, VISION

"The opposite of creativity is cynicism."

// ESA SAARINEN

"Creativity requires the courage to let go of certainties."

// ERICH FROMM

42

"Don't think. Thinking is the enemy of creativity. It's self-conscious, and anything self-conscious is lousy. You can't try to do things. You simply must do things."

// RAY BRADBURY

"The creative adult is the child who has survived." // URSULA K. LE GUIN

"Every act of creation is first an act of destruction." // PABLO PICASSO

YOU RE-DEFINE

CREATIVITY IS

CREATIVITY ISN'T

EXPERIENCES
& EMOTIONS

KNOWLEDGE
MISTAKES
CHOICES
DEPRESSION
CONTROL
ANGER
COURAGE
BEAUTY
ENRICHMENT
WHAT IS HAPPINESS?

FINDING CREATIVITY, HAPPINESS, AND THE ETERNAL TAO IN WISCONSIN

RW: *Tell me about Wisconsin.*

JV: Northwestern Wisconsin is my home. There is something about this place, the people, the lack of coasts—I can't explain it. I may never find a reason to leave.

RW: *How did the record* For Emma, Forever Ago *come about?*

JV: My best friends and I moved to North Carolina. We were very tight-knit—basically married to each other—but the move was really hard on me. I lost the sense of myself in our music. However, that year, I learned more than I had in any other year of my life. I had been sick with a liver infection and had gone through two hard breakups, one with those friends and another with a girlfriend. I got all my shit and moved back to Wisconsin into my dad's hunting cabin. I had considered quitting my music. I was teetering, but I had been working on some songs, all around this catalyst, "Flume." I'd never had a song quite like it; it was new. I was really isolated up there. I stayed for 3 months—writing and recording. I gained new confidences. My dad would swing by and drop off beer and apples.

RW: *Beer and apples? Yum. And what did you realize?*

JV: I'm weary of realization. One of the few things that I took away from the experience was that you are your only redeemer. You are the only one that has control over your own shit. I'd started down a cyclical path of darkness five or six years earlier, and I don't know how it happened—or why—but it had. I hadn't figured out how to get happy. I had forgotten somehow. This experience reconnected me to me.

RW: *That's like Carl Jung's concept of "Individuation."*

JV: I've always reacted to Jung in a really visceral way. My mom bought my dad *The Red Book* this past Christmas. It's wonderful. Jung is talking about things that he doesn't necessarily try to fully explain. I always think about Taoism when I think about Jung. He's talking about the connectivity between things, but he didn't try to connect every dot because he knew that we aren't ready for all the dots to be connected. For Jung, the "Oceanic feeling" is the best way to explain it. It's a notion that we are connected by a psyche and physical space. This knowing and unknowing reminds me of the first chapter of the *Tao De Ching*. It says:

> "THE TAO THAT CAN BE TOLD
> IS NOT THE ETERNAL TAO
> THE NAME THAT CAN BE NAMED
> IS NOT THE ETERNAL NAME."

RW: *How do these philosophies influence your work?*

JV: They inform and illuminate my creativity. Struggling with spiritual questions is important and rewarding, but if you think about heavy ideas like "I am; I'm not" all the time, it's pretty easy to either end up thinking about yourself too much or not enough. With creativity, it's important to not be self-important. Creativity is about unfurling into yourself—an act of becoming.

RW: *If you look at the major religions of the world, there is this paradox: To find yourself, you need to lose yourself. How does that relate to your music?*

JV: Every thought that I had since I moved to the cabin influenced the next. I wasn't afraid to be alone. I wanted to be happy. I didn't want to abuse my body past the point of it not being able to be my vehicle anymore. Bad thoughts breed bad thoughts. Good thoughts breed good thoughts. People like to look at life as some kind of singular event, but I think every moment is like water in a river. In Taoism, this is called *We Wei*—the Way of the Water. You look at the river—the water is constantly passing over the same stone. Movement and stillness. All part of the same motion and motionlessness.

RW: *Where are you now with your emotions?*

JV: I'm trying to make sure I don't lean on sadness again. It only serves as a crutch. I want to take the lessons I learned accessing my subconscious making the first record and do the same with an even clearer head. The songs I'm working on now sound different. Fuller and warmer. Less brittle. It takes a sand-painting patience. Some days I get real lonely. I don't have a girlfriend right now. But I live in Eau Claire. You can disappear here, but it's small enough where you'll always be accountable. I feel accounted for here.

RW: *SoulPancake is a great way to find a girlfriend.*

JV: That is the only reason I decided to talk with you, Rainn. That's how I roll.

// RAINN WILSON INTERVIEWS JUSTIN VERNON,
singer/songwriter and founding member of Bon Iver

"HE WHO CAN NO LONGER PAUSE TO WONDER AND STAND RAPT IN AWE, IS AS GOOD AS DEAD; HIS EYES ARE CLOSED." // **ALBERT EINSTEIN**

46

DIG DEEPER

WHAT WOULD YOU LIKE TO UNLEARN?
WHAT DO YOU WISH YOU KNEW MORE ABOUT?
WHAT'S ONE THING YOU HAD TO LEARN THE HARD WAY?

SOPHOPHOBIA
IS THE FEAR OF LEARNING

"THE MAIN THING IS TO PAY ATTENTION, PAY CLEAR ATTENTION TO EVERYTHING YOU SEE. NOTICE WHAT NO ONE ELSE NOTICES, AND YOU'LL KNOW WHAT NO ONE ELSE KNOWS."
// **LORIS HARROW,** *City of Ember*

WHAT'S ONE THING YOU LEARNED THAT
BLEW YOUR MIND?

AS YOU LEARN, YOUR BRAIN CREATES NEW SYNAPSES BETWEEN NEURONS. THE ADULT HUMAN BRAIN HAS A TOTAL OF 10 BILLION NEURONS IN THE CEREBRAL CORTEX ALONE, AND 60 TRILLION (YES, TRILLION) SYNAPSES.

SOURCE: *The Synaptic Organization of the Brain* **BY GORDON M. SHEPHERD (OXFORD UNIVERSITY PRESS, 1998)**

GREEK MATHEMATICIAN ARCHIMEDES DISCOVERED THE LAW OF HYDROSTATICS BY ACCIDENT IN THE PUBLIC BATHS OF SYRACUSE IN THE THIRD CENTURY B.C. HE THEN RAN NAKED FROM THE BATHS SHOUTING,

"EUREKA! EUREKA! I FOUND IT."

SOURCE: *Serendipity: Accidental Discoveries in Science* BY ROYSTON M. ROBERTS (WILEY, 1989)

A COLUMBIA UNIVERSITY STUDY SUGGESTS THAT THE GUILT WE OFTEN FEEL RIGHT AFTER MAKING "INDULGENT" CHOICES OR MISTAKES PASSES AS QUICKLY AS IT FLARES UP. HOWEVER, REGRETS OVER MISSED OPPORTUNITIES RARELY FADE; IN FACT, THEY INCREASE OVER TIME.

SOURCE: FOX NEWS

WHAT'S THE BIGGEST MISTAKES YOU'VE EVER MADE?

"WE DON'T LIKE THEIR SOUND, AND GUITAR MUSIC IS ON THE WAY OUT."
// DECCA RECORDING CO. REJECTING THE BEATLES IN 1962

"A MAN'S ERRORS ARE HIS PORTALS OF DISCOVERY."
// JAMES JOYCE

"IF AT FIRST YOU DON'T SUCCEED, TRY, TRY AGAIN. THEN QUIT. THERE'S NO POINT IN BEING A DAMN FOOL ABOUT IT."
// **W. C. FIELDS**

HOW DO YOU KNOW WHEN TO CALL IT QUITS AND WHEN TO ---- *FORGE AHEAD?*

"ONCE YOU LEARN TO QUIT, IT BECOMES A HABIT."
// **VINCE LOMBARDI**

IN THE 2000S, AN AVERAGE OF NEARLY 573,000 SMALL BUSINESSES OPENED ANNUALLY; 566,000 CLOSED THEIR DOORS EACH YEAR.
SOURCE: U.S. SMALL BUSINESS ADMINISTRATION

ON AVERAGE, COLLEGE GRADUATES EARN 80% MORE THAN HIGH SCHOOL GRADS. HOWEVER, TECH BILLIONAIRES BILL GATES AND STEVE JOBS ARE BOTH COLLEGE DROPOUTS. EAT THAT, IVY LEAGUE.

SOURCE: THE COLLEGE BOARD

 DIG DEEPER

WHAT DO YOU WISH YOU'D GIVEN UP SOONER?

WHAT WOULD YOU TRY IF YOU KNEW YOU COULDN'T FAIL?

WE COULDN'T THINK OF A THIRD QUESTION, SO, WELL, WE QUIT.

A LEDGE. A PERSON ON THE EDGE.

WHAT WOULD YOU SAY IF YOU HAD 60 SECONDS TO TALK A STRANGER OUT OF TAKING HIS OR HER LIFE?

"EVERYTHING CAN BE TAKEN FROM A MAN OR A WOMAN BUT ONE THING: THE LAST OF HUMAN FREEDOMS IS TO CHOOSE ONE'S ATTITUDE IN ANY GIVEN SET OF CIRCUMSTANCES, TO CHOOSE ONE'S OWN WAY." // **VIKTOR E. FRANKL**

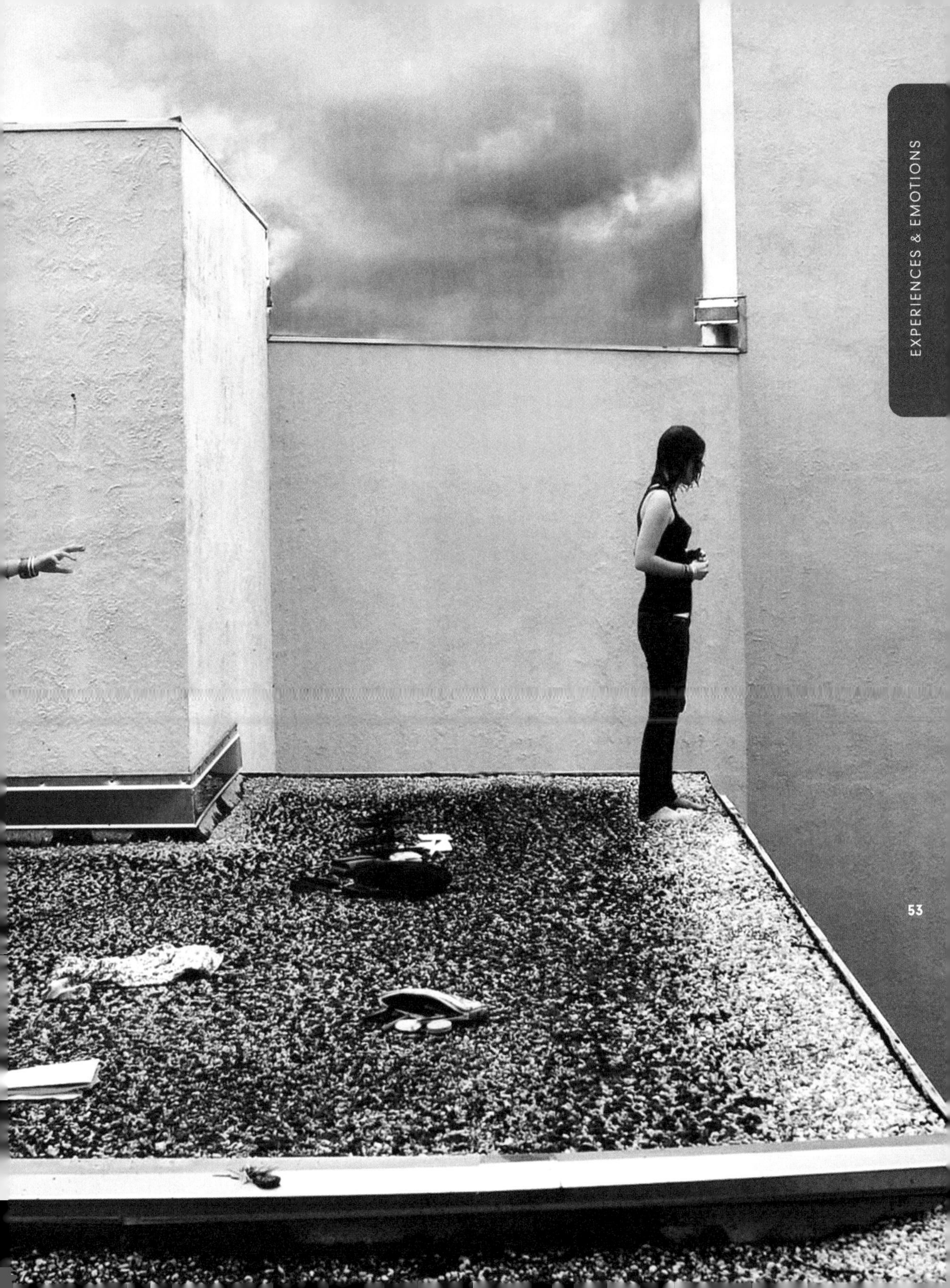

"IT IS IN THE NATURE OF ALL PASSIONATE AND UNCONTROLLED EMOTION TO PREY UPON AND WEAKEN THE FORCES OF REFLECTIVE POWER, AS MUCH AS IT IS IN THE NATURE OF CONTROLLED EMOTION TO STRENGTHEN THEM."
// **FROM** *The True Story of Guenever* **BY ELIZABETH STUART PHELPS**

WHAT EMOTION DO YOU WISH YOU COULD BETTER CONTROL?

IN TRADITIONAL CHINESE MEDICINE, HEALTH IS MANAGED BY TREATING THE SEVEN BASIC EMOTIONS. ANGER LIVES IN THE LIVER; WORRY IN THE SPLEEN; PENSIVENESS IN THE STOMACH; SADNESS IN THE LUNGS; FEAR IN THE KIDNEYS; AND JOY AND SHOCK BOTH AFFECT THE HEART.

SOURCE: HOWSTUFFWORKS.COM

"YOUR INTELLECT MAY BE CONFUSED, BUT YOUR EMOTIONS WILL NEVER LIE TO YOU."
// **ROGER EBERT**

A RECENT GALLUP POLL REPORTED THAT MOTORISTS WERE MORE WORRIED ABOUT ROAD RAGE (42%) THAN ABOUT DRUNK DRIVING (35%).

SOURCE: *New York Times*

 DIG DEEPER

WHY DOES REVENGE FEEL SO GOOD?

IS HAPPINESS A CHOICE?

WHAT EMOTIONS ARE YOU AFRAID OF?

"ANGER AS SOON AS FED IS DEAD. 'TIS STARVING MAKES IT FAT."
// EMILY DICKINSON

POP YOUR PROBLEMS

Ignoring your anger doesn't make it go away, so here's another approach to dealing with that pent-up angst.

STEP 1. Buy a bag of balloons.

STEP 2. Write something that makes you angry on each balloon.

STEP 3. Blow up the balloons. Catch your breath.

STEP 4. Find something sharp and start stabbing. Feel the release with every bang.

WHAT'S STOPPING YOU?

LIST 5 RISKS YOU HAVEN'T HAD THE GUTS TO TAKE YET.

01
_____

WHAT'S THE WORST THAT COULD HAPPEN? ....

02
_____

WHAT'S THE WORST THAT COULD HAPPEN? ....

03
_____

WHAT'S THE WORST THAT COULD HAPPEN? ....

04
_____

WHAT'S THE WORST THAT COULD HAPPEN? ....

05
_____

WHAT'S THE WORST THAT COULD HAPPEN? ....

 WARNING Don't take risks that break the law. They won't let you take this book to jail.

59

Beauty in the Bland

TO GET FROM ORDINARY TO EXTRAORDINARY TAKES A LITTLE ... EXTRA. AND WITH A LITTLE EXTRA EFFORT, YOU CAN FIND BEAUTY ANYWHERE.

"AND ABOVE ALL, WATCH WITH GLITTERING EYES THE WHOLE WORLD AROUND YOU BECAUSE THE GREATEST SECRETS ARE ALWAYS HIDDEN IN THE MOST UNLIKELY PLACES. THOSE WHO DON'T BELIEVE IN MAGIC WILL NEVER FIND IT." // **ROALD DAHL**

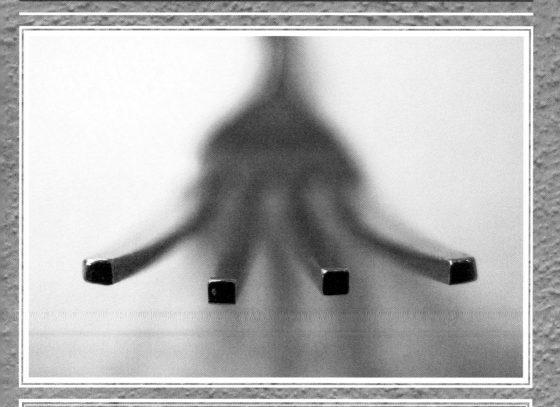

STEP 1

Pick up your camera.

STEP 2

Spend an entire day finding beauty hiding in the ordinary.

STEP 3

Create an extraordinary album.

61

DIG DEEPER

WHAT EXPERIENCE ARE YOU MOST LOOKING FORWARD TO IN LIFE?

DO YOUR EXPERIENCES USUALLY MATCH YOUR EXPECTATIONS?

WHAT SINGLE EXPERIENCE MOST TRANSFORMED YOU?

CAMERON CROWE'S DEBUT SCREENPLAY, *Fast Times at Ridgemont High*, WAS BASED ON THE YEAR HE SPENT POSING AS A STUDENT AT CLAIREMONT HIGH SCHOOL IN SAN DIEGO.

SOURCE: *San Francisco Chronicle*

IN A SURVEY OF STUDENTS STUDYING ABROAD, 97% SAID THE EXPERIENCE INCREASED THEIR MATURITY; 96% SAID IT INCREASED SELF-CONFIDENCE; 89% SAID IT ENABLED THEM TO TOLERATE AMBIGUITY; AND 95% SAID IT HAD A LASTING IMPACT ON THEIR WORLDVIEW.

SOURCE: INSTITUTE FOR THE INTERNATIONAL EDUCATION OF STUDENTS

"GOD WILL NOT LOOK YOU OVER FOR MEDALS, DEGREES, OR DIPLOMAS, BUT FOR SCARS."
// **ELBERT HUBBARD**

"A MIND THAT IS STRETCHED BY A NEW EXPERIENCE CAN NEVER GO BACK TO ITS OLD DIMENSIONS." // **OLIVER WENDELL HOLMES, JR.**

HAPPINESS

THEY DEFINE

HAP·PI·NESS | haˈpē-nəs | noun
1. good fortune; prosperity
2. **a)** a state of well-being and contentment; joy
   b) a pleasurable or satisfying experience
3. felicity, aptness

SYNONYMS
BEATITUDE, BLESSEDNESS, BLISS, CHEER, CHEERFULNESS, CHEERINESS, CONTENT, CONTENTMENT, DELECTATION, DELIGHT, DELIRIUM, ECSTASY, ELATION, ENCHANTMENT, ENJOYMENT, EUPHORIA, EXHILARATION, EXUBERANCE, FELICITY, GAIETY, GENIALITY, GLADNESS, GLEE, GOOD CHEER, GOOD HUMOR, GOOD SPIRITS, HILARITY, HOPEFULNESS, JOVIALITY, JOY, JUBILATION, LAUGHTER, LIGHTHEARTEDNESS, MERRIMENT, MIRTH, OPTIMISM, PARADISE, PEACE OF MIND, PLAYFULNESS, PLEASURE, PROSPERITY, REJOICING, SANCTITY, SEVENTH HEAVEN, VIVACITY, WELL-BEING

"Happiness is the meaning and the purpose of life, the whole aim and end of human existence." // **ARISTOTLE**

"MAYBE HAPPINESS IS SOMETHING WE CAN ONLY PURSUE, BUT NEVER HAVE." // **CHRIS GARDNER,** *The Pursuit of Happyness*

"THERE IS NEITHER HAPPINESS NOR MISERY IN THE WORLD; THERE IS ONLY THE COMPARISON OF ONE STATE TO ANOTHER, NOTHING MORE. HE WHO HAS FELT THE DEEPEST GRIEF IS BEST ABLE TO EXPERIENCE SUPREME HAPPINESS. WE MUST HAVE FELT WHAT IT IS TO DIE, THAT WE MAY APPRECIATE THE ENJOYMENTS OF LIFE."

// **ALEXANDRE DUMAS**

"If you observe a really happy man, you will find him building a boat, writing a symphony, educating his child, growing double dahlias or looking for dinosaur eggs in the Gobi Desert. He will not be searching for happiness as if it were a collar button that had rolled under the radiator, striving for it as a goal in itself. He will have become aware that he is happy in the course of living life 24 crowded hours of each day."

// **W. BERAN WOLFE**

64

"Happiness is nothing more than good health and a bad memory."
// **ALBERT SCHWEITZER**

YOU RE-DEFINE

HAPPINESS IS

HAPPINESS ISN'T

LOVE, SEX &
RELATIONSHIPS

LOVE

SEX

ATTRACTION

MARRIAGE

FAMILY

COMMUNICATION

MEN & WOMEN

STRANGERS

LOSS

WHAT IS A SOUL MATE?

ON FINDING YOUR SOUL MATE. AND SCHEDULING SEX.

I was sitting on the plane the other day watching this horrible romantic comedy when I started spontaneously crying. (Sorry, passenger in 11F.) Why? Because I sensed the connection between the two characters. I felt it. OK, I know. They're actors. But seeing their chemistry and being touched by it—that was as moving to me as sitting in a church pew singing hymns to God.

It reminds me of when I first met Jon. I felt something immediately. It was overpowering. And then ... dammit! He's married. Four years later, he was emailing around saying he was getting a divorce and looking for work elsewhere. So I replied and said, "Oh, that's funny because I had a really big crush on you. You should come to Los Angeles. I know a lot of people here. I have a spare room. A spare bed. In fact, spare room in my bed."

That night, I called my father and told him to write the name Jon Armstrong on his calendar. I told him, "Dad, this is the man I'm going to marry." Jon came to L.A. in 2001. We've been together ever since.

The thing is, I have no doubt that the universe wanted Jon and me to be together. I know he's my soul mate. He helps me see things differently, and I think I do the same for him. And that means it's worth it to us to work things out—not just on a material it's-important-for-the-kids level, but on a spiritual level. What does that mean? Well, I'm certainly not religious. And neither is Jon. But what I am is extraordinarily spiritual.

I define my spirituality by my connections to things around me, the emotions I feel when I read or hear something that moves me, and also, by being connected to other people and cherishing those relationships.

That's not to say our relationship doesn't have its bumps. It has bumps. Big bumps. One major bump happened after my first daughter was born. I didn't heal for a very long time, and we went without sex for 7 months. Yes, 7 months. We'd fall over into bed every night feeling victorious that we'd even made it to the end of the day. No sex.

We went to therapy because we were committed to working it out. And we had to learn that sex is also about timing. It's no longer going to be spontaneous-lovemaking-on-a-cliff-at-sunset-overlooking-the-sea. (Or even spontaneous-sex-on-the-couch-after-*Project-Runway*-and-pizza, for that matter.) You have to make time for it. Intimacy and sex are really important to a marriage. Now, it's still fun ... it's just *scheduled* fun.

I dated quite a bit in Los Angeles before we married, and I understand the ups and downs of dating—the "Oh, God! This is awful!" and the "Oh, God! Why on earth am I still committed to this relationship?" But let me tell you, when you're in the right relationship, there's nothing better.

Marry your best friend. Someone who constantly makes you laugh. Someone who will begin and end each day with a kiss. Someone who wants to make it work with you ... no matter what. Someone who moves you as if you were sitting in a church pew singing hymns to God.

// **HEATHER ARMSTRONG,** *creator of Dooce.com, professional blogger, author, mother*

67

68

IS UNCONDITIONAL LOVE A MYTH?

DO WE CHOOSE WHO WE LOVE?

CAN YOU TRULY LOVE A PERFECT STRANGER?

WHAT IS LOVE ?

"LOVE IS A SERIOUS MENTAL DISEASE." // **PLATO**

"LOVE IS OR IT AIN'T. THIN LOVE AIN'T LOVE AT ALL." // **TONI MORRISON**

SEX SELLS. APPARENTLY, SO DOES LOVE. THE LARGEST SEGMENT OF "PAID CONTENT" ON THE WEB IS PORNOGRAPHY. THE SECOND-LARGEST SEGMENT IS ONLINE DATING AND PERSONALS.

SOURCE: ONLINE PUBLISHERS ASSOCIATION

CHEMICALLY SPEAKING, "LOVE" IS AN INCREASE IN BLISS-INDUCING DOPAMINE (C_8-H_{11}-NO_2), BOOST IN HEARTBEAT-RACING NOREPINEPHRINE (C_8-H_{11}-NO_3), AND DECREASE IN SEROTONIN (C_{10}-H_{12}-N_2O), THAT FEISTY CHEMICAL THAT MAKES US OBSESS.

SOURCE: HOWSTUFFWORKS.COM

"SEX IS PART OF NATURE. I GO ALONG WITH NATURE." // **MARILYN MONROE**

DOES *sex* AFFE

2/3 OF COLLEGE STUDENTS HAVE BEEN IN A "FRIENDS WITH BENEFITS" RELATIONSHIP.
SOURCE: WAYNE STATE UNIVERSITY AND MICHIGAN STATE UNIVERSITY

"SEXUALITY IS FIRST AND FOREMOST THE WAY THAT GOD CHOOSES FOR US TO BE HERE ON EARTH, TO ENJOY THIS ENERGY OF LOVE IN THE PHYSICAL PLANE."
// **PAULO COELHO**

ONLY 5,000 SEMEN RELEASES SHOULD BE ALLOWED IN A LIFETIME TO MAINTAIN SPIRITUAL AND PHYSICAL HEALTH.
SOURCE: TRADITIONAL TAOIST DOCTRINE

T OUR SOULS

DIG DEEPER

IS SEX JUST AN ANIMAL IMPULSE?

WHAT'S THE RELATIONSHIP BETWEEN LOVE, SEX, AND INTIMACY?

WHAT DO YOU WISH YOU'D BEEN TAUGHT ABOUT SEX?

HOT FOR HUMILITY

LIST FIVE **NON-PHYSICAL** TRAITS THAT TURN YOU ON.

1. ....

   PLEASE ELABORATE.

   ....

2. ....

   PLEASE ELABORATE.

   ....

3. ....

   PLEASE ELABORATE.

   ....

4. ....

   PLEASE ELABORATE.

   ....

5. ....

   PLEASE ELABORATE.

   ....

73

"MODERN MARRIAGE. ONCE IT WAS 'SEE SOMEBODY, GET EXCITED, GET MARRIED.' NOW IT'S 'READ A LOT OF BOOKS, FENCE WITH A LOT OF FOUR-SYLLABLE WORDS, AND PSYCHOANALYZE EACH OTHER UNTIL YOU CAN'T TELL THE DIFFERENCE BETWEEN A PETTING PARTY AND A CIVIL SERVICE EXAM.'" // **STELLA**, *Rear Window*

WHY DO MARRIAG

WE DON'T SEEM TO LEARN OUR LESSONS, EVEN THE SECOND TIME AROUND. 43% OF FIRST MARRIAGES END IN DIVORCE; 67% OF SECOND MARRIAGES MEET THE SAME FATE. AMONG THE FACTORS BELIEVED TO BE ASSOCIATED WITH A HIGHER DIVORCE RATE ARE COHABITATION PRIOR TO MARRIAGE AND INFREQUENT CHURCH ATTENDANCE.

SOURCE: NATIONAL CENTER FOR HEALTH STATISTICS

"WHEN ENTERING INTO A MARRIAGE, ONE OUGHT TO ASK ONESELF: DO YOU BELIEVE YOU ARE GOING TO ENJOY TALKING WITH THIS WOMAN UP INTO YOUR OLD AGE? EVERYTHING ELSE IN MARRIAGE IS TRANSITORY, BUT MOST OF THE TIME YOU ARE TOGETHER WILL BE DEVOTED TO CONVERSATION." // **FRIEDRICH NIETZSCHE**

SO MANY
S FAIL?

DIG DEEPER

WHAT'S THE BEST PREPARATION FOR MARRIAGE?   IS DIVORCE A FAILURE?   IS MARRIAGE OUTDATED?

A SURVEY OF DIVORCED COUPLES FOUND THAT 70% REPORTED THE CAUSE OF THEIR DIVORCE AS FALLING IN ONE OF THESE FIVE CATEGORIES: INCOMPATIBILITY, LACK OF EMOTIONAL SUPPORT, ABUSE, SEXUAL PROBLEMS, AND MONEY.

SOURCE: CALIFORNIA STATE UNIVERSITY, SACRAMENTO

"IT'S A FUNNY THING COMING HOME. NOTHING CHANGES. EVERYTHING LOOKS THE SAME, FEELS THE SAME, EVEN SMELLS THE SAME. YOU REALIZE WHAT'S CHANGED IS YOU."
// **BENJAMIN BUTTON,** *The Curious Case of Benjamin Button*

"A GREAT PART OF THE PLEASURE OF TRAVEL LIES IN THE FULFILLMENT OF EARLY WISHES TO ESCAPE THE FAMILY." // **SIGMUND FREUD**

DOES YOUR FAMILY SEE THE REAL YOU?

THERE ARE NEARLY 90 GROUPS ON FACEBOOK ADVOCATING FOR KEEPING PARENTS OFF THE SITE. THE "DUDE, YOUR MOM FRIEND REQUESTED ME? (STUDENTS AGAINST PARENTS W/ FACEBOOK)" GROUP IS ONE OF THE LARGEST, WITH MORE THAN 1,500 MEMBERS. GOOD THING YOU CAN UNFRIEND PEOPLE.

SOURCE: FACEBOOK

ABOUT ONE-THIRD OF TEENAGERS ADMIT TO USING THEIR CELL PHONES TO CHEAT DURING SCHOOL. ONLY 3% OF PARENTS BELIEVED THEIR CHILD WOULD USE A CELL PHONE TO CHEAT.

SOURCE: COMMON SENSE MEDIA

DIG DEEPER WHAT DO YOU HIDE FROM YOUR FAMILY?   HOW DO YOU BECOME FRIENDS WITH YOUR FAMILY?
DO YOU EVER STOP CARING ABOUT WHAT YOUR PARENTS THINK OF YOU?

Pen Pal on the D.L.

Now that everything's hyper-digitized, it's no wonder we
think WTF? (in a good way) when we get a real letter.
In the mail. Addressed to us. In ink. On paper. With an
actual stamp. Who's up for a revival?

STEP 1

Jumpstart a secret pen-pal relationship with
someone you see all the time.

STEP 2

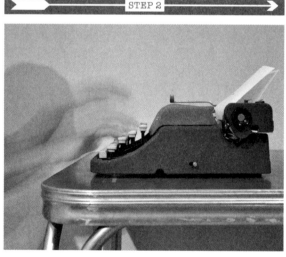

Write him or her a letter. Ask for a reply.

"A hidden connection is stronger than an obvious one." // Heraclitus of Ephesus

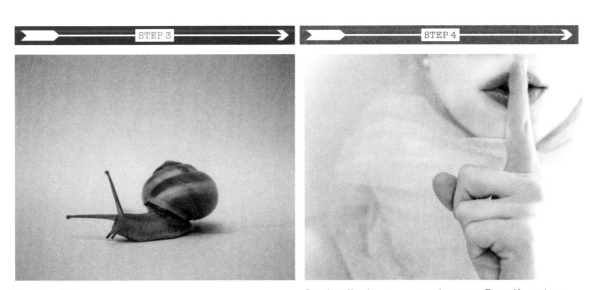

STEP 3

Snail mail it.

STEP 4

Don't talk about your exchanges. Ever. Keep 'em on the down-low.

IN A STUDY CONDUCTED BY THE *Journal of Social and Personal Relationships*, 62% OF PROFESSIONAL MEN AND WOMEN REPORT THAT SEXUAL TENSION IS PRESENT IN THEIR CROSS-GENDER FRIENDSHIPS.

SOURCE: *Psychology Today*

AT SOME POINT DURING THE RUN OF THE TV SERIES *Friends*, EACH OF THE SIX MAIN CHARACTERS WAS ROMANTICALLY INTERESTED IN ANOTHER CHARACTER. YES, EVEN PHOEBE.

SOURCE: AN AVID *Friends* **FAN**

 DIG DEEPER   HOW IS ATTRACTION BORN?   WHAT CAN YOU LEARN FROM THE OPPOSITE SEX?
HOW DO YOU KNOW IF A FRIENDSHIP IS HEALTHY?

CAN MEN AND WOMEN REALLY BE *"just friends"?*

"PERHAPS MORE THAN ANY OTHER RELATIONSHIP, FRIENDSHIPS BETWEEN MEN AND WOMEN ARE ALIVE WITH AMBIGUITY, CONTRADICTION, ENERGY, PARADOX." // **CELIA ALLISON HAHN**

"FRIENDS ARE GENERALLY OF THE SAME SEX, FOR WHEN MEN AND WOMEN AGREE, IT IS ONLY IN THEIR CONCLUSIONS; THEIR REASONS ARE ALWAYS DIFFERENT." // **GEORGE SANTAYANA**

WE DOUBLE-SHOT DARE YOU

. . . .

"Be not forgetful to entertain strangers: for thereby some have entertained angels unawares." // **FROM** *Hebrews 13:2*, **KING JAMES BIBLE**

. . . .

Next time you're out getting your daily caffeine fix, offer to pay for the person in line behind you. Bond over your mutual addiction.

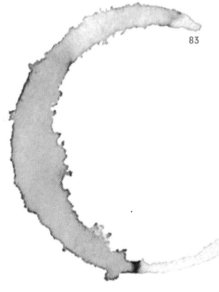

83

GOOD GRIEF

"The risk of love is loss, and the price of loss is grief. But the pain of grief is only a shadow when compared with the pain of never risking love."

// HILARY STANTON ZUNIN

IT'S MORBID, BUT EYE-OPENING:
Put on your finest black and crash a funeral.
Without an emotional connection to the deceased,
observe love manifesting itself as grief.

SOUL MATE

THEY DEFINE

SOUL·MATE | sōl·māt | noun

1. a person who is perfectly suited to another in temperament

2. a person who strongly resembles another in attitudes or beliefs

> **SYNONYMS**
> ALTER EGO, COMPANION, CONFIDANTE, FRIEND, HEART'S DESIRE, HELPMATE, KINDRED SOUL, KINDRED SPIRIT, LOVER, ONE'S PROMISED, PARTNER, TRUE LOVE

"LOVE ISN'T FINDING A PERFECT PERSON. IT'S SEEING AN IMPERFECT PERSON PERFECTLY." // **SAM KEEN**

"A soul mate doesn't have to be a sex mate." // LISA GEE

SEAN   *Do you have a soul mate?*

WILL   *Define that.*

SEAN   *Someone you can relate to, someone who opens things up for you.*

WILL   *Sure, I got plenty.*

SEAN   *Well, name them.*

WILL   *Shakespeare, Nietzsche, Frost, O'Connor.*

// **SEAN MAGUIRE AND WILL HUNTING,** *Good Will Hunting*

86   "THE MINUTE I HEARD MY FIRST LOVE STORY I STARTED LOOKING FOR YOU, NOT KNOWING HOW BLIND THAT WAS. LOVERS DON'T FINALLY MEET SOMEWHERE. THEY'RE IN EACH OTHER ALL ALONG." // **JALAL AD-DIN MUHAMMAD RUMI**

"PEOPLE THINK A SOUL MATE IS YOUR PERFECT FIT, AND THAT'S WHAT EVERYONE WANTS. BUT A TRUE SOUL MATE IS A MIRROR, THE PERSON WHO SHOWS YOU EVERYTHING THAT IS HOLDING YOU BACK, THE PERSON WHO BRINGS YOU TO YOUR OWN ATTENTION SO YOU CAN CHANGE YOUR LIFE." // **ELIZABETH GILBERT**

YOU RE-DEFINE

SOUL MATE IS   SOUL MATE ISN'T

VIRTUES & VICES

HATE
GENEROSITY
GREED
DETACHMENT
SACRIFICE
GOSSIP
HUMOR
LYING
ACCOUNTABILITY
WHAT IS EVIL?

A FOUR-STEP PROGRAM TO FINDING EUDEMONIA (A.K.A. FLOURISHMENT)

Step 1. Get to the core of your trauma.

Trauma is the health problem of our time, along with addiction. Abandonment, abuse, neglect—everything is related to trauma.

The way I think about it is that even if I could correct the biological problem in a person's system, he or she would still have a spiritual disease. There is never going to be a single biological bullet that will correct addiction or conquer trauma. There is always something else going on, some spiritual malady.

When we experience trauma, we initially have a fight or flight response, but what most people don't realize is that we flip from sympathetic to para-sympathetic responses. Something we share with other mammals such as opossums. Our autonomic nervous system flips from hyperexcitation to hyperinhibition. We freeze. In that freeze state, we begin to dissociate from our emotions. And in those dissociated states, other things can emerge—rage, anger, hate. We have to rebuild that ■■■■■■ity to regulate our emotions, which is why I call sobriety "slow-briety." The brain has to rewire itself—and that takes time.

Step 2. Recognize that a vice is not a weakness.

Reality is a state of being, but your feelings about reality are another matter. Addicts are trying to escape those feelings. It's a new biological disorder that is so profoundly human—the diseased brain says, "I don't need help. I can go to the bar instead."

That's when a vice becomes problematic—when it takes control and disrupts the balance of our health. I don't classify things as "good" or "bad," "virtue" or "vice." I think "healthy" or "unhealthy." Vices are activities that may not be unhealthy on their own, but are definitely unhealthy when used to combat a trauma.

We call that weakness. But it's not. It's possibly frailness, but the people who are stuck in their vices or addictions are not weak. In fact, they are an unusually strong and rich population who show how profoundly strong they are

during their recoveries. They become the people they are meant to be without the liabilities.

Step 3. Find ways to be of service.

Ultimately, the highest order that humans have is empathy—the ability to use the body as an antenna to absorb, appreciate, and to tune into another person's feelings. That is a very powerful exchange. That is true intimacy—a virtue that we've lost in our country and culture.

It was actually DJ AM who taught me about service. He was on my talk show and had on a great pair of Nikes. I said they looked cool, and the next day, he showed up with a pair for me. I was so touched. He said, "It's my pleasure to do this for you today. Thank you for keeping me sober by allowing me to be of service." I'll never forget that. The simplest acts of giving and gratitude make us healthy. You want to pass it on.

Step 4. Achieve eudemonia.

Gratitude and service are virtues—practices that bring good things to life. I tend to adhere to Aristotelian principles that real happiness comes from living a good life. It's not necessarily a life filled with extreme arousal and moments of "Yahoo! I'm so happy" but something more nurturing, substantial, and real.

It's eudemonia. Aristotle felt that everything progresses toward an ultimate need. Fire goes up. Rocks go down. We Westerners think our need must be orgasmic joy and happiness all the time. My heroin addicts feel that way when they take that first hit. But that's the greatest example of how feeling really good is not real happiness.

Instead, eudemonia is about flourishing—that's the way philosophers have recently translated it. It's about being nurturing, fulfilled, and creating a meaningful life.

89

// **AS TOLD TO RAINN WILSON BY DR. DREW,** *a radio/ television personality, board-certified internist, addiction medicine specialist, host of the nationally syndicated talk show* Loveline, *and producer of VH1's* Celebrity Rehab

"HATE IS TOO GREAT A BURDEN TO BEAR.
IT INJURES THE HATER MORE THAN IT
INJURES THE HATED." // **CORETTA SCOTT KING**

DIG DEEPER

DOES HATE AFFECT OUR PHYSICAL WELL-BEING?
WHAT'S THE BEST WAY TO HANDLE HATE?
WHAT EXPRESSION OF HATE HAS MOST AFFECTED YOU?

VIRTUES & VICES

"PASSIONATE HATRED CAN GIVE MEANING AND PURPOSE TO AN EMPTY LIFE." // **ERIC HOFFER**

WHY DO WE HATE?

MEMBERSHIP IN THE KU KLUX KLAN PEAKED AT 6 MILLION PEOPLE IN 1924. TODAY, THERE ARE 150 KLAN CHAPTERS, AND THEIR ROSTER HAS DWINDLED TO FEWER THAN 8,000 MEMBERS.

SOURCE: FBI

91

ANTI-MUSLIM HATE CRIMES ROSE BY MORE THAN 50% FROM 2003 TO 2004. INCIDENTALLY, THE IRAQ WAR BEGAN WHEN THE UNITED STATES INVADED IRAQ ON MARCH 20, 2003.

SOURCE: THE PLURALISM PROJECT AT HARVARD UNIVERSITY

REVERSE PICKPOCKET

ADMIT IT: GIVING GIFTS IS FUN BECAUSE GETTING THANKED FEELS GREAT. BUT PERHAPS REAL GENEROSITY IS ACTUALLY THE ACT OF ANONYMOUS GIVING. LET'S GO FOR IT.

STEP 1	PULL OUT THE BIGGEST BILL IN YOUR WALLET.
STEP 2	STASH THE CASH IN AN ENVELOPE LABELED **"YOU'VE BEEN TAGGED BY A SOULPANCAKE REVERSE PICKPOCKET."**
STEP 3	SLIP THE LOOT INTO THE BAG OF A STRANGER. IF YOU'RE FEELING BOLD, AIM FOR THE BACK POCKET.
STEP 4	DON'T GET CAUGHT. IT WOULD BE REALLY AWKWARD.

"REAL GENEROSITY IS DOING SOMETHING NICE FOR SOMEONE WHO WILL NEVER FIND OUT." // **FRANK A. CLARK**

"I THINK IT ALL COMES BACK TO BEING VERY SELFISH AS AN ARTIST. I MEAN, I REALLY DO JUST WRITE AND RECORD WHAT INTERESTS ME."
// **DAVID BOWIE**

94

DURING SEX, THE FEMALE PRAYING MANTIS SOMETIMES BITES OFF THE HEAD OF HER PARTNER IN ORDER TO MAKE HIS MOVEMENTS MORE VIGOROUS.

SOURCE: *Animal Planet*

"TO BE SUCCESSFUL YOU HAVE TO BE SELFISH, OR ELSE YOU NEVER ACHIEVE. AND ONCE YOU GET TO YOUR HIGHEST LEVEL, THEN YOU HAVE TO BE UNSELFISH."
// **MICHAEL JORDAN**

DIG DEEPER

WHAT IS GREED?

WHAT IS IT OK TO BE ATTACHED TO?

HOW DO YOU KEEP YOUR WANTS FROM IMPOSING ON THE RIGHTS OF OTHERS?

SELFISH?

THE JOHNS HOPKINS COMPARATIVE NONPROFIT SECTOR PROJECT ESTIMATES THAT CHARITABLE GIVING IN THE UNITED STATES WAS 1.85% OF THE SIZE OF THE ECONOMY IN RECENT YEARS; IT WAS AS LITTLE AS 0.13% IN GERMANY. BY THIS RECKONING, THEN, GERMANS ARE 99.87% SELFISH, AND AMERICANS ARE MORE THAN 98% SELFISH.

SOURCE: SLATE.COM

"HE WHO WOULD BE SERENE AND PURE NEEDS BUT ONE THING, DETACHMENT."
// MEISTER ECKHART

URGE TO PURGE

WE'RE ALL GUILTY OF HOARDING—CLOSETS, DESKS, AND DASHBOARDS FULL OF CLOTHES, PAPERS, AND PILES. IT'S TIME TO SEPARATE YOURSELF FROM YOUR STUFF. AND NOT LOOK BACK.

YOUR MISSION: GET RID OF SOMETHING (OR A STACK OF SOMETHINGS) THAT YOU SHOULD HAVE THROWN OUT A LONG TIME AGO. REPEAT AS NECESSARY.

CAREFULLY LIST 5 THINGS
YOU WOULD LITERALLY CHOP OFF YOUR LITTLE TOE FOR.

01

PLEASE ELABORATE

02

PLEASE ELABORATE

03

PLEASE ELABORATE

04

PLEASE ELABORATE

05

PLEASE ELABORATE

DISCLAIMER SoulPancake is not responsible for any bodily injuries sustained while reading this book. Hold on to your toes. Please.

"BE LESS CURIOUS ABOUT PEOPLE AND MORE CURIOUS ABOUT IDEAS."
// **MARIE CURIE**

WHY ARE WE OBSESSED WITH TALKING ABOUT OTHER PEOPLE?

CELEBRITY GOSSIP BLOG PEREZHILTON.COM GETS MORE THAN 7 MILLION PAGE VIEWS PER DAY.

SOURCE: QUANTCAST.COM

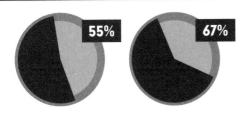

GOSSIP ACCOUNTS FOR 55% OF MEN'S
CONVERSATION TIME AND 67% OF WOMEN'S.
SOURCE: SOCIAL ISSUES RESEARCH CENTRE

DIG DEEPER

DOES TALKING ABOUT OTHER PEOPLE HELP US
UNDERSTAND THE COMPLEXITY OF BEING HUMAN?

IS IT GOSSIP IF WHAT YOU ARE SAYING IS TRUE?

WHEN HAVE YOU REGRETTED TALKING ABOUT
SOMEONE BEHIND THEIR BACK?

"BACKBITING QUENCHETH THE LIGHT OF THE HEART, AND EXTINGUISHETH THE LIFE
OF THE SOUL." // **BAHÁ'U'LLÁH**

this piece:

20¢

this piece:

10¢

this piece:

10¢

free sample

"THE MOST WASTED OF ALL DAYS IS ONE WITHOUT LAUGHTER."
// E. E. CUMMINGS

WHAT PASSES FOR HUMOR ON THE WALLS OF PUBLIC RESTROOMS CAN LEAVE YOU FEELING LIKE THE HUMAN RACE NEEDS ITS MOUTH WASHED OUT WITH SOAP. LET'S INJECT SOME FUN INTO THE FILTH.

 # BATHROOM HUMOR

STEP 1. FIND A PUBLIC RESTROOM WITH PAPER TOWEL DISPENSERS, NOT THOSE LOUD BLOW DRYER THINGS.

STEP 2. WRITE OR DRAW SOMETHING ON A PAPER TOWEL TO GIVE THE NEXT PERSON A GOOD, CLEAN LAUGH.

STEP 3. WASH YOUR HANDS. TWICE.

> "MAKE THE LIE BIG, MAKE IT SIMPLE, KEEP SAYING IT, AND EVENTUALLY THEY WILL BELIEVE IT."
> // **ADOLF HITLER**

> "WITH LIES, YOU MAY GO FORWARD IN THE WORLD, BUT YOU MAY NEVER GO BACK." // **GRINKO,** *Transsiberian*

WHAT'S ONE *lie* YOU'RE GLAD YOU TOLD?

DIG DEEPER

WHAT'S ONE LIE YOU WISH YOU HADN'T TOLD?

WHAT LIE HAS CAUSED YOU THE MOST HARM?

SHOULD WE LIE TO PROTECT OTHER PEOPLE'S FEELINGS?

ONE OF THE THREE MOST COMMON METHODS USED BY EMPLOYEES TO GET A RAISE IS TO BLUFF ABOUT AN OFFER FROM A COMPETING FIRM. TRY THIS AT YOUR OWN RISK.

SOURCE: EHOW.COM

A STUDY BY THE UNIVERSITY OF MASSACHUSETTS FOUND THAT 60% OF PEOPLE LIE AT LEAST ONCE DURING A NORMAL 10-MINUTE CONVERSATION. WOMEN MOST OFTEN LIE TO MAKE OTHERS FEEL BETTER. MEN MOST OFTEN LIE TO MAKE THEMSELVES FEEL BETTER.

SOURCE: *Journal of Basic and Applied Social Psychology*

"IT IS BETTER TO CONQUER YOURSELF THAN TO WIN A THOUSAND BATTLES. THEN THE VICTORY IS YOURS. IT CANNOT BE TAKEN FROM YOU, NOT BY ANGELS OR BY DEMONS, HEAVEN OR HELL." // **BUDDHA**

WHICH OF YOUR FLAWS MOST BOTHERS YOU?

HOW ARE YOU A HYPOCRITE?

WHAT'S ONE THING YOU'RE GLAD YOU DIDN'T DO?

> "IT IS NOT ONLY WHAT WE DO, BUT ALSO WHAT WE DO NOT DO, FOR WHICH WE ARE ACCOUNTABLE." // **MOLIÈRE**

HOW DO YOU KEEP YOURSELF IN CHECK?

WHEN PRESENTED WITH DNA EVIDENCE ALONE, 25% OF DEFENDANTS WILL CONFESS TO THE CRIME.
SOURCE: THE INNOCENCE PROJECT

GMAIL'S "GOGGLE" FEATURE PREVENTS THE INTOXICATED FROM SENDING EMBARRASSING LATE-NIGHT E-MAILS. WHEN ACTIVATED, THE PROGRAM FORCES A USER TO SOLVE A SERIES OF MATH PROBLEMS BEFORE ALLOWING ANY MESSAGE TO BE SENT. NOW IF ONLY THEY COULD STOP US FROM DRUNK DIALING AND "SEXTING" AS WELL.

SOURCE: GOOGLE

EVIL

THEY DEFINE

E·VIL | ē-vəl | adjective

1. a) morally reprehensible; sinful, wicked
   b) arising from actual or imputed bad character or conduct
2. a) inferior
   b) causing discomfort or repulsion; offensive
   c) disagreeable
3. a) causing harm; pernicious
   b) marked by misfortune
   c) unlucky

"Evil is whatever distracts." // **FRANZ KAFKA**

"IF ONLY THERE WERE EVIL PEOPLE SOMEWHERE INSIDIOUSLY COMMITTING EVIL DEEDS AND IT WERE NECESSARY ONLY TO SEPARATE THEM FROM THE REST OF US AND DESTROY THEM. BUT THE LINE DIVIDING GOOD AND EVIL CUTS THROUGH THE HEART OF EVERY HUMAN BEING. AND WHO IS WILLING TO DESTROY A PIECE OF HIS OWN HEART?" // **ALEXANDER SOLZHENITSYN**

"… all the qualities and admirable perfections of man, are purely good, and exist. Evil is simply their nonexistence. So ignorance is the want of knowledge; error is the want of guidance; forgetfulness is the want of memory; stupidity is the want of good sense. All these things have no real existence." // **'ABDU'L-BAHÁ**

"What is evil? Killing is evil, lying is evil, slandering is evil, abuse is evil, gossip is evil: envy is evil, hatred is evil, to cling to false doctrine is evil; all these things are evil. And what is the root of evil? Desire is the root of evil, illusion is the root of evil." // **BUDDHA**

108

SYNONYMS

ANGRY, ATROCIOUS, BAD, BANEFUL, BASE, BEASTLY, CALAMITOUS, CORRUPT, DAMNABLE, DEPRAVED, DESTRUCTIVE, DISASTROUS, EXECRABLE, FOUL, HARMFUL, HATEFUL, HEINOUS, HIDEOUS, INIQUITOUS, INJURIOUS, LOATHSOME, LOW, MALEFICENT, MALEVOLENT, MALICIOUS, MALIGNANT, NEFARIOUS, NO GOOD, OBSCENE, OFFENSIVE, PERNICIOUS, POISON, RANCOROUS, REPROBATE, REPUGNANT, REPULSIVE, REVOLTING, SPITEFUL, STINKING, UGLY, UNPLEASANT, UNPROPITIOUS, VICIOUS, VILE, VILLAINOUS, WICKED, WRATHFUL, WRONG

"THE WORLD IS A DANGEROUS PLACE, NOT BECAUSE OF THOSE WHO DO EVIL, BUT BECAUSE OF THOSE WHO LOOK ON AND DO NOTHING." // ALBERT EINSTEIN

YOU RE-DEFINE

EVIL IS

EVIL ISN'T

INTROSPECTION,
REFLECTION &
IDENTITY

SELF-IMAGE

EGO

SECRETS

MEDITATION

RIGHT & WRONG

INTUITION

FAITH

AWARENESS

TRANQUILITY

WHAT IS PRAYER?

MEDITATION = TURNING GARBAGE INTO GOLD

The phrase that got me meditating was, "True happiness is not out there; true happiness lies within." I would think about this phrase and although it had a ring of truth, the phrase gives no indication of where the "within" is, nor does it tell a person how to get there. One day it struck me that perhaps meditation was the way to go within. After reading and asking many people questions about a whole slew of different forms of meditation, I finally chose Maharishi Mahesh Yogi's Transcendental Meditation as the technique I wanted to use to go within.

Transcendental Meditation is a mental technique, an ancient form of meditation, brought back for this time by Maharishi Mahesh Yogi. It is a unique form of meditation—easy and effortless, yet supremely profound. It is not concentration, nor contemplation, nor hypnotism, nor imagining. In Transcendental Meditation, you're given a mantra and taught how to use it. Maharishi's mantra turns the awareness 180 degrees within.

Normally, our awareness is always pointed out, out, out. We look for happiness out there. Now during meditation the awareness is directed within. And one, naturally, dives through subtler levels of mind, subtler levels of intellect—and at the border of intellect, we transcend and experience the source of thought. It is so natural because each deeper level of mind and intellect has more happiness and so we're just pulled happily to the transcendent.

The source of thought is the same source of everything that is a thing. The Source. The Transcendent. Ocean of Pure Totality of Consciousness. Modern Science's Unified Field. Being. The Absolute. The Self. Totality. The Reality. Many, many names for this field.

This field of the transcendent is unbounded, infinite and eternal consciousness. It is beyond the field of relativity, beyond duality. It is oneness. This field of pure consciousness has infinite qualities. It is intelligence, creativity, happiness, bliss, universal love, energy, and dynamic peace. It is an all-positive field. There is no negativity here in the same way there is no darkness in the brightest light.

Everything that is a thing has emerged from this field of pure consciousness. What is missing in our lives these days is the experience of this deepest level of life, this ocean of pure bliss. When a person truly experiences this, when a person truly transcends, this person can begin to expand his or her consciousness. He begins to unfold his full potential as a human being, and the result is breathtaking. All that negativity he's been carrying around begins to recede. Things like anxiety, tension, stress, sorrow, depression, hate, anger, and fear begin to lift away, which is a great relief.

Through this process of regular meditation, you could say that a person is cleaning the machine of garbage and infusing it with gold. Life will truly get better and better and better. And it all comes from within. We just need a technique to get there and have that experience. Awareness of all this is fine, but it's the experience of meditation that truly brings about enlightenment.

With today's advanced brain research, doctors can see on an EEG machine, that when a person truly transcends, the full brain lights up, it is wholly engaged. They call this Total Brain Coherence. Any other thing we do utilizes smaller different parts of the brain, but here is an experience that utilizes the entire brain. This phenomenon truly tells us what a profound relationship there is between the human being's brain and nervous system and the field of the transcendent.

It is said that mankind was not made to suffer, that bliss is our nature. In our world, we do find some happiness, but we notice that because it is a world of change, that happiness can fade, and soon we're looking somewhere else for it. Don't let yourself forget that this happiness found within is the only kind that just grows and grows. So the phrase is true: True happiness is not out there; true happiness lies within.

// **DAVID LYNCH,** *filmmaker, practitioner of Transcendental Meditation, and founder of the David Lynch Foundation for Consciousness-Based Education and World Peace*

111

"I PAINT SELF-PORTRAITS BECAUSE I AM SO OFTEN ALONE, BECAUSE I AM THE PERSON I KNOW BEST." // FRIDA KAHLO

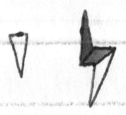

SCRAP PAPER PORTRAIT

WE'RE OBSESSED WITH HOW THE WORLD SEES US. WE STRIVE TO APPEAR SMART, CONFIDENT, GENEROUS, AMBITIOUS . . . BUT HOW DO WE SEE OURSELVES?

113

STEP 1. GRAB A PIECE OF SCRAP PAPER.

STEP 2. SKETCH A SELF-PORTRAIT THAT SUMS UP <u>THE REAL YOU.</u>

STEP 3. STICK IT IN THIS BOOK.

SIGMUND FREUD'S THEORY OF PSYCHOANALYSIS DIVIDES THE HUMAN PSYCHE INTO THREE PARTS: 1) THE UNCONSCIOUS ID, WHICH ACTS STRICTLY TO SEEK PLEASURE OR AVOID PAIN; 2) THE EGO, WHICH SEEKS REALISTIC WAYS TO BENEFIT THE ID'S DRIVE IN THE LONG TERM; 3) THE SUPEREGO, WHICH AIMS FOR PERFECTION AND INCLUDES THE INDIVIDUAL'S IDEALS, SPIRITUAL GOALS, AND CONSCIENCE.

SOURCE: *An Outline of Psycho-analysis* BY SIGMUND FREUD

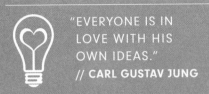

"EVERYONE IS IN LOVE WITH HIS OWN IDEAS."
// **CARL GUSTAV JUNG**

"BE WHO YOU ARE AND SAY WHAT YOU FEEL BECAUSE THOSE WHO MIND DON'T MATTER AND THOSE WHO MATTER DON'T MIND." // **DR. SEUSS**

How can you be confident without being EGOTISTICAL?

115

WHAT'S YOUR BIGGEST FLAW? // WHAT'S YOUR GREATEST STRENGTH? // WHAT HELPS YOU KEEP YOUR EGO IN CHECK?

RECENT RESEARCH IN LEARNING AND INDIVIDUAL DIFFERENCES SUGGESTS THAT TEENAGE STUDENTS WHO ARE OVERCONFIDENT HAVE LOWER READING COMPREHENSION THAN STUDENTS WHO ARE UNDER-CONFIDENT. IN ALL 34 COUNTRIES STUDIED, STUDENTS WHO WERE OVERCONFIDENT WERE MORE APT TO TEST BELOW THEIR COUNTRY'S AVERAGE ON READING SCORES.

SOURCE: *Los Angeles Times*

STASH-A-SECRET*

We've all fantasized about standing on a giant podium with a megaphone and surround sound to confess our deepest, darkest secrets. Ah, the release. You can almost feel it. (Or maybe that's the *moo goo gai pan*.) Either way, it's time to overcome your fears of being misunderstood or judged. Put your secret out there—just in a quieter way.

STEP 1 ➡	STEP 2 ➡

Think it.

Think of that one secret sitting heavy in your gut.

Write it.

Write it on a scrap of paper.

116

---

* **"SECRET"** From the Latin **secernere** (**se**—"apart" + **cernere**—"to sift"). It means to separate or distinguish.

> "NOTHING MAKES US SO LONELY
> AS OUR SECRETS."
> // **DR. PAUL TOURNIER**

→ STEP 3 →

Stash it.

Go to a bookstore and slip it into another copy of the *SoulPancake* book.

→ STEP 4 →

Flee the scene.

Enjoy the release of having a perfect stranger help carry your load.

117

ASK AND YE ~~SHALL~~ MAY OR MAY NOT RECEIVE

LIST FIVE OF YOUR PRAYERS THAT HAVEN'T BEEN
ANSWERED . . . YET.

1

2

3

4

5

"WITHOUT EVIL THERE COULD BE NO GOOD, SO IT MUST BE GOOD TO BE EVIL SOMETIMES."
// **SATAN,** *South Park: Bigger, Larger & Uncut*

HOW HAS YOUR SENSE OF RIGHT AND WRONG EVOLVED?

120

DIG DEEPER

WHEN IS IT IMPORTANT TO REBEL?
WHAT WILL YOU NEVER CHANGE YOUR MIND ABOUT?
WHAT HAVE YOU UNLEARNED SINCE CHILDHOOD?

"ARE RIGHT AND WRONG CONVERTIBLE TERMS, DEPENDENT UPON POPULAR OPINION?" // **WILLIAM LLOYD GARRISON**

139 COUNTRIES (NEARLY 72% OF ALL COUNTRIES IN THE WORLD) HAVE ABOLISHED THE DEATH PENALTY IN LAW OR PRACTICE. ON AVERAGE, IN THE PAST DECADE, THREE OR MORE COUNTRIES A YEAR ABOLISH THE DEATH PENALTY FOR ALL CRIMES.
SOURCE: AMNESTY INTERNATIONAL

121

ANTHROPOLOGISTS SAY HUMAN SACRIFICE IS A RITUAL PRACTICED IN A STABLE SOCIETY AND CAN BE CONDUCIVE TO ENHANCING SOCIETAL BONDS. BUT WITHOUT CIVIL ORDER, HUMAN SACRIFICE CAN ALSO RESULT IN OUTBURSTS OF "BLOOD FRENZY" AND MASS KILLINGS THAT DESTABILIZE SOCIETY. ACCORDING TO THE *2009 Guinness World Records*, THE THUGGEE CULT IN INDIA, WHICH RITUALLY PRACTICED HUMAN SACRIFICE, WAS RESPONSIBLE FOR APPROXIMATELY 2 MILLION DEATHS.
SOURCE: *The Independent*

A UNIVERSITY OF SOUTHERN CALIFORNIA STUDY OF BRAIN-DAMAGED PATIENTS WHO COULD ONLY USE DELIBERATE REASONING, NOT EMOTIONAL INTUITION, IN THEIR DECISION-MAKING PROCESS FOUND THAT "THEY ENDED UP DOING SUCH A COMPLICATED ANALYSIS, FACTORING EVERYTHING IN, THAT IT COULD TAKE THEM HOURS TO DECIDE BETWEEN TWO KINDS OF CEREAL."

SOURCE: *Psychology Today*

WHAT'S ONE TIME YOU WISH YOU HAD TRUSTED YOUR GUT? WHY DIDN'T YOU?

"WE ARE ALL SELFISH AND I NO MORE TRUST MYSELF THAN OTHERS WITH A GOOD MOTIVE." // GEORGE GORDON, LORD BYRON

"TRUST YOURSELF. YOU KNOW MORE THAN YOU THINK YOU DO." // DR. BENJAMIN SPOCK

IN *Blink*, POP SOCIOLOGIST MALCOLM GLADWELL SUGGESTS THAT GUT INSTINCTS ARE UNCONSCIOUS, RATIONAL DECISIONS MADE RAPIDLY IN THE FIRST TWO SECONDS OF THOUGHT.

SOURCE: GLADWELL.COM

123

 DIG DEEPER HOW DO YOU KNOW WHEN YOU'VE MADE THE RIGHT DECISION? WHAT'S THE DIFFERENCE BETWEEN INSTINCT AND INTUITION? HOW MUCH DO YOU TRUST YOURSELF?

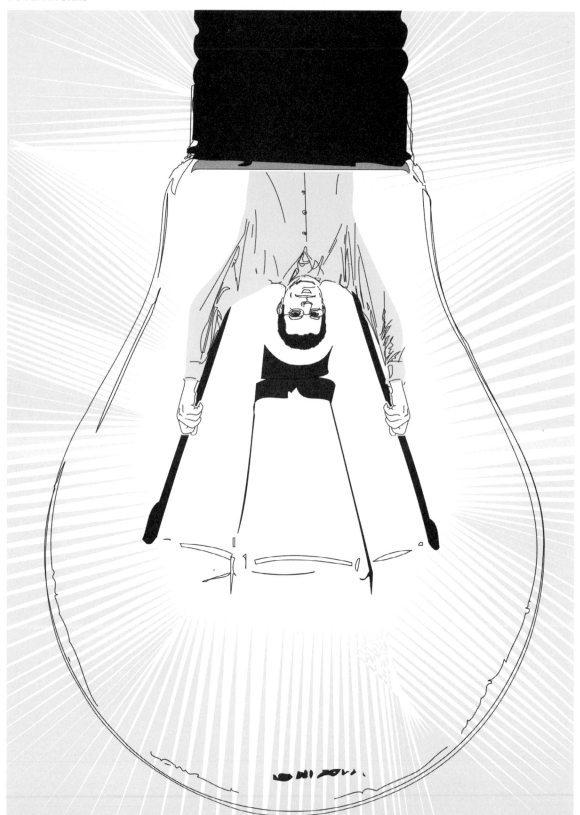

"OUR DOUBTS ARE TRAITORS, / AND MAKE US LOSE THE GOOD WE OFT MIGHT WIN / BY FEARING TO ATTEMPT ..."
// **FROM** *Measure for Measure*
BY WILLIAM SHAKESPEARE

"DOUBT IS HUMBLE AND THAT IS WHAT MAN NEEDS TO BE, CONSIDERING THAT HUMAN HISTORY IS JUST A LITANY OF GETTING SHIT DEAD WRONG."
// **BILL MAHER,** *Religulous*

DO YOU HAVE TO EXPERIENCE DOUBT BEFORE YOU CAN REACH CERTAINTY?

125

DIG DEEPER

IS THERE ANYTHING THAT SHOULD NEVER BE QUESTIONED?
WHY IS IT SO HARD TO HAVE FAITH?
WHAT CAN WE LEARN FROM OTHER PEOPLE'S DOUBTS?

RESEARCH INDICATES THAT MORE THAN 40% OF BRIDES HAVE WEDDING ANXIETY. INTERESTINGLY, THE TERM "COLD FEET" ORIGINALLY MEANT "WITHOUT MEANS OR RESOURCES," REFERRING TO A 1605 PLAY WHERE A CHARACTER WAS TOO POOR TO BUY SHOES. TODAY, THE TERM HAS EVOLVED TO MEAN "ANXIETY AND UNCERTAINTY ABOUT AN UNDERTAKING TO THE POINT OF WITHDRAWING."

SOURCE: ASSOCIATED CONTENT

THE CERTAINTY EFFECT (OR ALLAIS PARADOX) IS ONE OF THE MOST IMPORTANT UTILITY THEORIES IN THE BEHAVIORAL AND SOCIAL SCIENCES. IT HOLDS THAT, GIVEN TWO OPTIONS, PEOPLE TEND TO SELECT THE SAFER CHOICE—THE ONE WITH A HIGHER CERTAINTY OF A GOOD OUTCOME—EVEN THOUGH THE OTHER MAY BE MORE REWARDING.

SOURCE: *Econometrica*

MUTE YOUR MOUTH

CEASE YOUR CHATTER. DON'T SPEAK FOR AN ENTIRE DAY. JUST LISTEN.

DESCRIBE YOUR EXPERIENCE

"IN THE ATTITUDE OF SILENCE THE SOUL FINDS THE PATH IN A CLEARER LIGHT, AND WHAT IS ELUSIVE AND DECEPTIVE RESOLVES ITSELF INTO CRYSTAL CLEARNESS." // MAHATMA GANDHI

A RECENT STUDY IN THE ARCHIVES OF GENERAL PSYCHIATRY FOUND THAT ABOUT 10% OF AMERICANS, OR 27 MILLION PEOPLE, TAKE ANTIDEPRESSANTS. THAT'S TWICE AS MANY AS A DECADE EARLIER.

SOURCE: *USA Today*

NATURAL HEALERS SAY A DIET RICH IN CAYENNE, FENNEL, HAWTHORN BERRIES, PARSLEY, AND ROSEMARY CAN COMBAT HIGH BLOOD PRESSURE AND "CALM THE NERVES."

SOURCE: *Prescription for Nutritional Healing* BY PHYLLIS A. BALCH (AVERY, 2000)

WHAT DO YOU DO TO FIND CALM IN A CHAOTIC WORLD?

DIG DEEPER

WHO COOLS YOUR CRAZY? // WHAT DOES IT MEAN TO BE IN THE MOMENT? // WHEN DO YOU FEEL MOST REFLECTIVE?

"BASICALLY, I'M FOR ANYTHING THAT GETS YOU THROUGH THE NIGHT—BE IT PRAYER, TRANQUILIZERS, OR A BOTTLE OF JACK DANIEL'S." // **FRANK SINATRA**

"I DON'T KNOW ANYONE HERE WHO GOES TO CHURCH WHEN HE'S HAD A ROUGH DIVORCE OR IS GOING THROUGH DEPRESSION. WE GO OUT INTO NATURE INSTEAD." // **BJÖRK**

129

PRAYER

PRAYER | prer | noun

1. **a)** an address (as a petition) to God or a god in word or thought
   b) a set order of words used in praying
   c) an earnest request or wish
2. the act or practice of praying to God or a god
3. a religious service consisting chiefly of prayers
4. something prayed for
5. a slight chance

SYNONYMS
APPEAL, APPLICATION, BEGGING, BENEDICTION, BESEECHING, COMMUNION, DEVOTION, ENTREATY, GRACE, IMPLORATION, IMPLORING, IMPRECATION, INVOCATION, LITANY, ORISON, PETITION, PLEA, PLEADING, REQUEST, REQUEST FOR HELP, ROGATION, SERVICE, SUIT, SUPPLICATION, WORSHIP

"**Pray,** v.: To ask that the laws of the universe be annulled on behalf of a single petitioner confessedly unworthy."

// AMBROSE BIERCE

"MOST PEOPLE DO NOT PRAY; THEY ONLY BEG."

// GEORGE BERNARD SHAW

"PRAYER IS NOT AN OLD WOMAN'S IDLE AMUSEMENT. PROPERLY UNDERSTOOD AND APPLIED, IT IS THE MOST POTENT INSTRUMENT OF ACTION." // MAHATMA GANDHI

"PRAYER IS ONLY ANOTHER NAME FOR GOOD, CLEAN, DIRECT THINKING."

// MR. GRUFFYDD, *How Green Was My Valley*

"There is nothing in the world so much like prayer as music is."

// WILLIAM P. MERRILL

YOU RE-DEFINE

PRAYER IS

PRAYER ISN'T

131

GOD &
RELIGION

TALKING ABOUT GOD
UNITY OF RELIGION
RELIGIOUS DOCTRINE
DOUBT
NECESSITY OF RELIGION
WORSHIP
EVOLUTION & CREATIONISM
HEAVEN & HELL
TALKING TO GOD
WHAT IS GOD?

THE BUDDHA, THE JEW-DDHA, AND THE SEARCH FOR MEANING

RAINN: *So let me lead off with this: What is the meaning of life?*

HAROLD: Viktor Frankl says life has no inherent meaning, which is a bleak prospect for a lot of people. But it's completely consistent for me, not only with existential psychology, which I subscribe to, but it's also a deeply held Buddhist principle that it's up to us to create meaning. Frankl's premise is we seek meaning; it's our nature to do so.

Almost anyone who has achieved a fair measure of their original goals is left with that feeling of despair—is that all there is?—and that feeling of discovery, a glimpse of the wisdom that says there is much more to life. So I go with that.

RAINN: *My search for meaning renewed once I had achieved what I set out to do, which was be a working actor. I got there, and I felt kinda hollow.*

HAROLD: I think most people feel that. They remain mired in that search for what they think will make them happy. You'll never get what you need because it's not possible.

RAINN: *Are you about to quote the Rolling Stones?*

HAROLD: Ha. No. The Buddha.

RAINN: *What would the Buddha say?*

HAROLD: That we're suffering beings. It's our nature. We suffer from the want of what we don't have. The fear of losing what we do have. We are acquisitive; we're grasping. We're attached to our desires. I finish one good meal, and I'm thinking about the next one. I receive some praise or reward, and now I want more. We are engaged in this process for the rest of our lives. And there's no ending ... until your last breath.

RAINN: *I will say, you look like the Jew-ddha.*

HAROLD: I feel that way. Jewish Buddhism has become a trend. There's an amazing statistic that Jews are only 2.5% of the American population, but Jewish participation in Buddhist groups ranges from 6% up to 30% .

RAINN: *Why do you think Buddhism and Judaism correlate so well?*

HAROLD: I think for philosophical, secular-leaning Jews, God is a construct, not necessarily an active spiritual presence. One thing I have observed is all the major religions are reforms. Buddhism is a reform of Hinduism. A lot of the Buddhist cultures that were laid on that Hindu culture still have the imagery, the idolatry. Islam was an overlay of a pagan religion. People were walking around the *qaaba*, the sacred stone in Mecca, for time immemorial. They were already making the pilgrimage long before Muhammad came along. And Christianity is reformed Judaism. People don't throw away their old religions; they build and extend them. What they throw out is an old, corrupt bureaucracy.

RAINN: *And what is art in this world view? Why do we express ourselves through humor?*

HAROLD: There are so many pat analyses of humor. For instance, people always start laughing at somebody farting.

RAINN: *I've heard that the fart is the most universal humor. Even Eskimos have 50 words for fart.*

HAROLD: So let's take the fart as a metaphor for our vulnerability. The accidental revelation of our humanity.

RAINN: *I accidentally reveal myself about 40 times a day. You can ask my wife.*

HAROLD: And that's what good comedy does. It bypasses the intellect and touches us where we're most human. It's a reflex in the diaphragm, an instinct like fear.

RAINN: *So why do we create?*

HAROLD: It seems like human ingenuity is endless. It's hardwired in who we are—this need to create and affect our world in some way.

RAINN: *I think the act of creating art is the same act as worship—we're here in the material world, and our toenails are growing and we smell. Yet we're never quite satisfied because we long for something more—transcendence.*

HAROLD: In a way, all art was originally some worshipful recreation. The amount of art that got poured into the churches in celebration of God; it's a great inspiration to people. In our secular world, there is still something magical about that process. The attempt to define or evoke the human experience in a universal way—it's a spiritual pursuit.

RAINN: *How are you spiritual without believing in God per se?*

HAROLD: I don't deny that we live in a miraculous world, and it's driven by forces we may never understand. And that's awesome. It's mysterious. But I don't give it a name. I don't pretend to understand it. I have no problem with God, but making God an entity is not important for me.

RAINN: *Let me ask this: Who would win in a wrestling match? You or Ivan Reitman?*

HAROLD: I can take Ivan. He's a big baby.

// RAINN WILSON INTERVIEWS HAROLD RAMIS,
actor, director, writer, and Jew-ddha

133

"Who is God?" [Search]

WAS THE MOST GOOGLED QUESTION IN 2007.
SOURCE: *Google Year-End Zeitgeist 2007.*
PEW INTERNET & AMERICAN LIFE PROJECT

THE WORLD'S FIRST INSTANCE OF TECHNOLOGICAL
COMMUNICATION INCLUDED THE WORD "GOD."
SAMUEL MORSE'S TELEGRAPH IN 1844 READ:

"WHAT HATH GOD WROUGHT?"

WHY IS TALKING ABOUT GOD SO

AWKWARD?

DIG
DEEPER

WHERE SHOULD TALKING ABOUT GOD BE STRICTLY OFF-LIMITS?
WITH WHOM WOULD YOU WANT TO HAVE A REAL CONVERSATION ABOUT GOD?
WHAT TOPICS DO YOU WISH WERE A LITTLE LESS TABOO?

"IF YOU TALK TO GOD, YOU ARE PRAYING. IF GOD TALKS TO YOU, YOU HAVE SCHIZOPHRENIA." // **THOMAS S. SZASZ**

"MOVE OUT OF YOUR COMFORT ZONE. YOU CAN ONLY GROW IF YOU ARE WILLING TO FEEL AWKWARD AND UNCOMFORTABLE WHEN YOU TRY SOMETHING NEW." // **BRIAN TRACY**

135

"FREETHINKERS ARE THOSE WHO ARE WILLING TO USE THEIR MINDS WITHOUT PREJUDICE AND WITHOUT FEARING TO UNDERSTAND THINGS THAT CLASH WITH THEIR OWN CUSTOMS, PRIVILEGES, OR BELIEFS. THIS STATE OF MIND IS NOT COMMON, BUT IT IS ESSENTIAL FOR RIGHT THINKING." // **LEO TOLSTOY**

MOST PEOPLE WOULD AGREE THAT THE DECISION TO DISLIKE SOMETHING BEFORE EXPERIENCING IT IS A TOTAL COP-OUT. AND WE'RE ALL GUILTY OF IT, WHETHER IT'S AVOCADOS, COUNTRY MUSIC, OR EVEN RELIGION. BUT CAN YOU SAY WITH 100% CONVICTION THAT YOU'RE OPPOSED TO SOMETHING IF YOU HAVEN'T ACTUALLY TRIED IT?

DON'T KNOCK IT 'TIL YOU TRY IT

STEP 1. LOOK UP ALL THE PLACES IN YOUR CITY WHERE PEOPLE GET THEMSELVES SOME GOD. AND YES, WE MEAN ALL—BE IT A MOSQUE, CHURCH, SYNAGOGUE, TEMPLE, YOGA STUDIO, OR MEDITATIVE DRUM CIRCLE.

STEP 2. MAP OUT A PLAN TO VISIT THESE APPROACHES TO WORSHIP.

STEP 3. JUST WALK IN. (IF YOU'RE SCARED OF THE CONVERT-OR-ELSE CROWD, RECRUIT A WINGMAN.)

STEP 4. OPEN YOUR THIRD EYE AND SEE WHAT YOU FIND.

137

GUESS WHAT? WALKING ON WATER IS POSSIBLE AFTER ALL. MIX 200 GALLONS OF WATER, 1,000 POUNDS OF CORNSTARCH, AND SOME BLUE FOOD COLORING, AND YOU'LL GET A NON-NEWTONIAN, LIQUID-LIKE SUBSTANCE THAT TURNS INTO A SOLID WHEN WALKED UPON.

SOURCE: *MythBusters*

WHAT IS SCRIPTURE? 33% SAY IT'S THE WORD OF GOD, LITERALLY TRUE WORD FOR WORD; 30% SAY IT'S THE WORD OF GOD, BUT NOT LITERALLY TRUE; 28% SAY IT'S WRITTEN BY MEN AND NOT THE WORD OF GOD; 9% DON'T KNOW.

SOURCE: *2009 U.S. Religious Landscape Survey,* **THE PEW FORUM ON RELIGION & PUBLIC LIFE**

How literally should we interpret religious texts?

"THE LETTER OF SCRIPTURE IS A VEIL JUST AS MUCH AS IT IS A REVELATION; HIDING WHILE IT REVEALS, AND YET REVEALING WHILE IT HIDES." // **ANDREW JUKES**

DIG DEEPER

IS THERE AN EXPIRATION DATE ON SCRIPTURE? WHO IS BEST EQUIPPED TO INTERPRET RELIGIOUS TEXTS? SHOULD RELIGIOUS LAWS EVOLVE?

"WOE TO THE MAKERS OF LITERAL TRANSLATIONS, WHO BY RENDERING EVERY WORD WEAKEN THE MEANING! IT IS INDEED BY SO DOING THAT WE CAN SAY THE LETTER KILLS AND THE SPIRIT GIVES LIFE." // **VOLTAIRE**

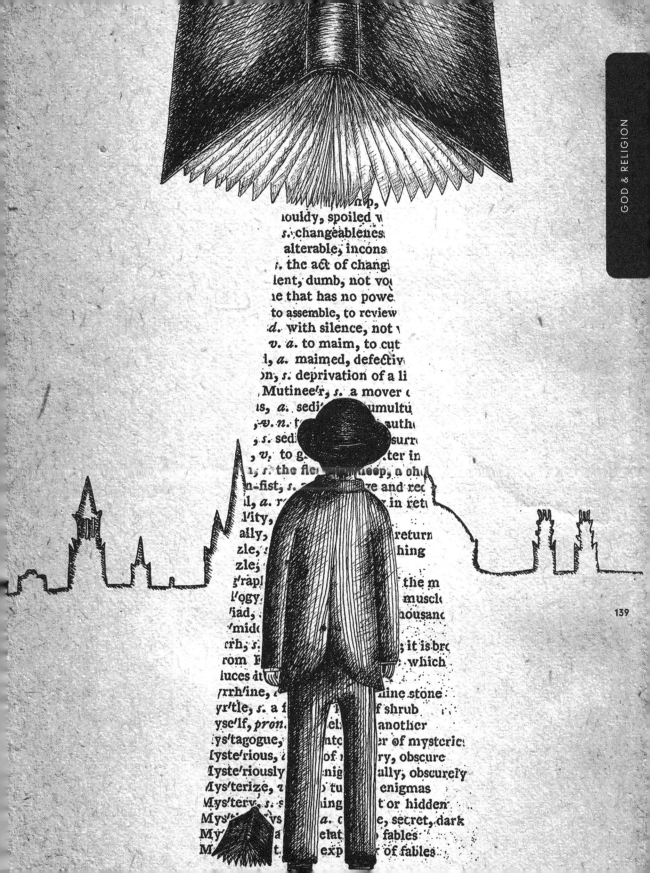

139

THE UNITED NATIONS HUMAN RIGHTS COUNCIL IS NOT ALLOWED TO JUDGE RELIGIONS. SPECIFICALLY, CRITICISM OF SHARIA LAW OR *fatwas* IS NOW FORBIDDEN.

SOURCE: INTERNATIONAL HUMANIST AND ETHICAL UNION

WHAT DO YOU DO WHEN YOU **CAN'T** WRAP YOUR HEAD AROUND CERTAIN TEACHINGS IN YOUR RELIGION?

140

"SKEPTICISM IS THE BEGINNING OF FAITH."
// OSCAR WILDE

"ONE'S FIRST STEP IN WISDOM IS TO QUESTION EVERYTHING—AND ONE'S LAST IS TO COME TO TERMS WITH EVERYTHING."
// GEORG CHRISTOPH LICHTENBERG

A SURVEY CONDUCTED BY THE CENTER FOR APPLIED RESEARCH IN THE APOSTOLATE AT GEORGETOWN UNIVERSITY FOUND THAT 74% OF CATHOLICS BELIEVE MARRIED MEN SHOULD BE ORDAINED AS PRIESTS.

SOURCE: *USA Today*

141

 DIG DEEPER

WHICH RELIGIOUS LAWS DO YOU STRUGGLE WITH—AND WHY?
WHAT ONE THING WOULD YOU LIKE TO CHANGE ABOUT YOUR RELIGION?
IF YOU COULD ASK GOD ONE QUESTION, WHAT WOULD IT BE?

DO WE NEED RELIGION?

DIG DEEPER

HAS RELIGION DONE MORE HARM THAN GOOD?
WHAT RELIGION WOULD YOU JOIN IF YOU HAD TO PICK ONE?
CAN YOU HAVE A RELATIONSHIP WITH GOD WITHOUT RELIGION?

THE OLDER YOU ARE, THE MORE LIKELY RELIGION IS TO BE VERY IMPORTANT TO YOU. THAT'S THE SENTIMENT FOR BETWEEN 60% AND 70% OF ADULTS OVER THE AGE OF 50, AS OPPOSED TO 44% OF ADULTS UNDER THE AGE OF 30.

SOURCE: THE PEW RESEARCH CENTER

ON THE ROLE OF RELIGION IN ONE'S LIFE:

 **56%** VERY IMPORTANT

 **26%** SOMEWHAT IMPORTANT

 **16%** NOT IMPORTANT

SOURCE: *2009 U.S. Religious Landscape Survey,*
THE PEW FORUM ON RELIGION & PUBLIC LIFE

143

"WE HAVE JUST ENOUGH RELIGION TO MAKE US HATE, BUT NOT ENOUGH TO MAKE US LOVE ONE ANOTHER."
// **JONATHAN SWIFT**

"MEN DESPISE RELIGION BECAUSE THEY SIMULTANEOUSLY HATE IT AND ARE AFRAID IT MAY BE TRUE." // **BLAISE PASCAL**

WHAT DO YOU WORSHIP?

LIST FIVE THINGS YOU DEVOTE YOURSELF TO.

1

HOW DO YOU SHOW YOUR DEVOTION? _____

_____

2

HOW DO YOU SHOW YOUR DEVOTION? _____

_____

3

HOW DO YOU SHOW YOUR DEVOTION? _____

_____

4

HOW DO YOU SHOW YOUR DEVOTION? _____

_____

5

HOW DO YOU SHOW YOUR DEVOTION? _____

_____

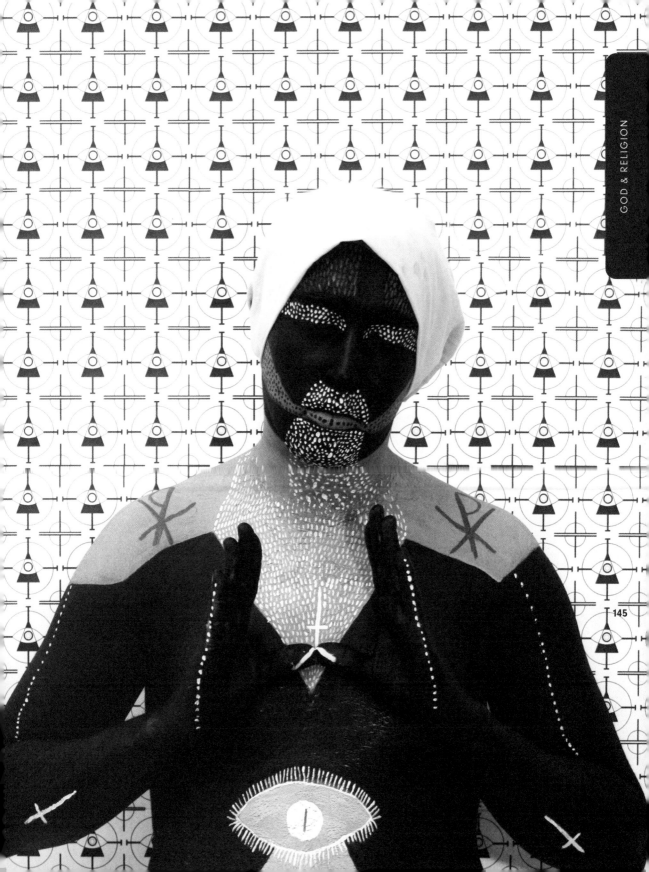

145

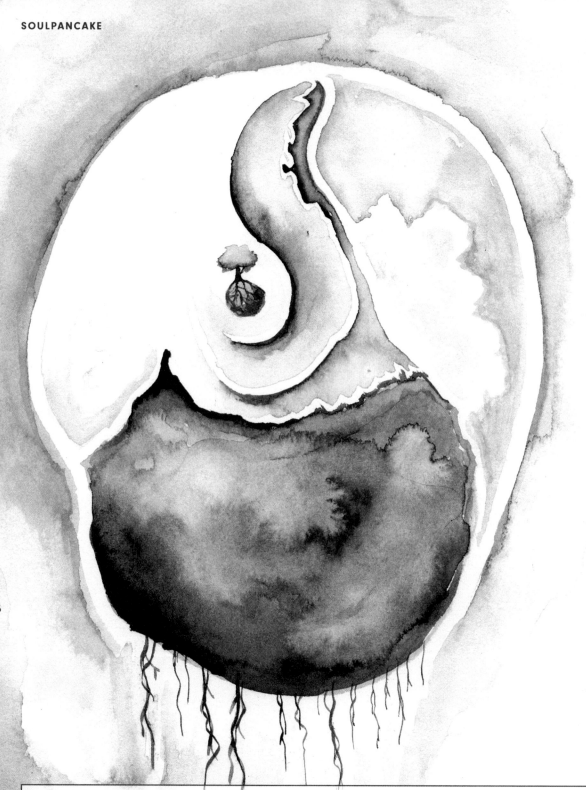

"IF WE ARE GOING TO TEACH CREATION SCIENCE AS AN ALTERNATIVE TO EVOLUTION, THEN WE SHOULD ALSO TEACH THE STORK THEORY AS AN ALTERNATIVE TO BIOLOGICAL REPRODUCTION." // **JUDITH HAYES**

65% NO. OF AMERICANS WHO FAVOR TEACHING CREATIONISM ALONGSIDE EVOLUTION IN SCHOOLS.

SOURCE: CBS NEWS

"IN ORDER TO MAKE AN APPLE PIE FROM SCRATCH, YOU MUST FIRST CREATE THE UNIVERSE."
// **CARL SAGAN**

AN ANALYSIS OF MITOCHONDRIAL DNA CONDUCTED BY THE ROYAL INSTITUTE OF TECHNOLOGY IN STOCKHOLM FOUND THAT 95% OF MODERN DOGS EVOLVED FROM A HANDFUL OF WOLVES DOMESTICATED IN EAST ASIA ABOUT 15,000 YEARS AGO.

SOURCE: *New Scientist*

HOW DID WE GET HERE?

 DIG DEEPER

IS IT POSSIBLE THAT EVOLUTION AND CREATIONISM DON'T NECESSARILY CANCEL EACH OTHER OUT? IF WE EVOLVE PHYSICALLY, CAN WE ALSO EVOLVE SPIRITUALLY? WHAT DOES SCIENCE FAIL TO EXPLAIN FOR YOU?

"THE FRONTIER BETWEEN HELL AND HEAVEN IS ONLY THE DIFFERENCE BETWEEN TWO WAYS OF LOOKING AT THINGS." // **GEORGE BERNARD SHAW**

HAIKU HEREAFTER

WHETHER YOU THINK HEAVEN
AND HELL ARE METAPHORS,
FIGMENTS OF THE HUMAN
IMAGINATION, OR ACTUAL
DESTINATIONS COMPLETE
WITH HARPS AND HELLFIRE,
SUM THEM UP IN HAIKU FORM.
(YOU KNOW THE DRILL—TRIM
DOWN THE SYLLABLES:
FIVE-SEVEN-FIVE.)

149

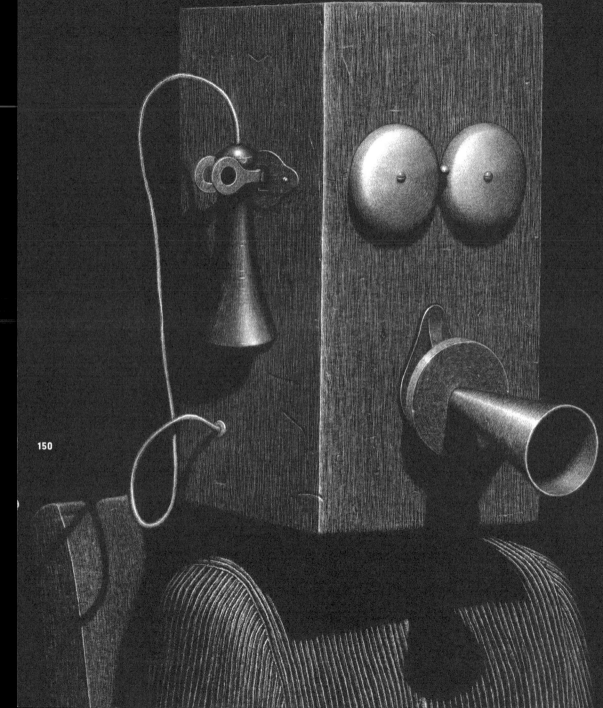

FORGET
◆ THE ◆
FORMALITIES

Wouldn't it be great if you could just pick up the phone and call the "Creator"? Here's your chance.

DIAL 925-BUZZ-GOD

Speak your mind. Just keep it snappy. Even God hates rambling voicemails.

151

"GOD REMAINS ON SPEAKING TERMS WITH EVERYBODY."
// **REVEREND MR. CARMICHAEL,** *Shanghai Express*

GOD

GOD | gäd | noun

1. the supreme or ultimate reality; the Being perfect in power, wisdom, and goodness who is worshipped as creator and ruler of the universe
2. a being or object believed to have more than natural attributes and powers and to require human worship; specifically, one controlling a particular aspect or part of reality
3. a person or thing of supreme value
4. a powerful ruler

SYNONYMS

ABSOLUTE BEING, ALL KNOWING, ALL POWERFUL, ALLAH, ALMIGHTY, CREATOR, DIVINE BEING, FATHER, GOD, HOLY SPIRIT, INFINITE SPIRIT, JAH, JEHOVAH, KING OF KINGS, LORD, MAKER, YAHWEH, DEITY, DEMIGOD, DEMON, DIVINITY, HOLINESS, IDOL, MASTER, NUMEN, OMNIPOTENT, POWER, PRIME MOVER, PROVIDENCE, SOUL, SPIRIT, TOTEM, TUTELARY, UNIVERSAL LIFE FORCE, WORLD SPIRIT

"I cannot believe in a God who wants to be praised all the time." // **FRIEDRICH NIETZSCHE**

"GOD THINKS WITHIN GENIUSES, DREAMS WITHIN POETS, AND SLEEPS WITHIN THE REST OF US."

// **PETER ALTENBERG**

"GOD IS JUST AN *imaginary friend* FOR GROWN-UPS."

// **WALTER CREWES,** *The Big Bounce*

"PEOPLE SEE GOD EVERY DAY, THEY JUST DON'T RECOGNIZE HIM."

// **PEARL BAILEY**

"God is not a cosmic bellboy for whom we can press a button to get things done." // **HARRY EMERSON FOSDICK**

152

YOU RE-DEFINE

GOD IS

GOD ISN'T

SCIENCE &
TECHNOLOGY

FOUR THINGS I'VE LEARNED ABOUT IDEAS

1. Innovators get to decide which new (and old) ideas matter—and that's OK.

When we talk about innovation, we immediately think of new ideas. But maybe innovation is about making old ideas new. I did an interview with [former U.S. Senator] Chuck Hagel once where he said that we have to change how we think about innovation—because not all old ideas are bad ones. Look at cell phones. Telephone communication is actually a very old idea, but Steve Jobs brought something new to it with the iPhone. And now Apple gets to decide what is innovative in cell phones.

If you look at Internet innovation, it's the same thing. There's this giant ecosystem that has been around for years with the potential to make the world a better place. We as users get to decide which different kinds of ideas we choose to consume or not consume—and that's what innovators will use to decide what to develop.

2. Technology must be infused with compassion so that it can achieve its purpose of empowering people.

What often gets lost in most conversations about technology is that technology needs to be infused with kindness, compassion, and love. Not popular words when you are sitting in a corporate boardroom. What do I mean by that? We are all complicated, flawed people. But I do believe people are inherently good, so it's important to do good things with technology.

Take, for example, the conversation about Internet brutality—about victims and perpetrators online. There are discussions about whether we should regulate the Internet as a public utility. That's polarizing. Instead, we need to bring people together to build supportive communities. The challenge for all of us when we seek to create good things is admitting that we can't do it alone.

Technology should be used as a tool for the disenfranchised. If we think of it this way, it makes it much easier to decide where to put our energies. We have to ask ourselves: What are we doing with our time? What are the conversations that we want to have everyday? And how will this serve people?

3. Without good communication, powerful ideas will fail to turn into reality.

To get science, technology, and spirituality to mesh, you have to start with communication. If people don't understand a powerful idea, then they can't adopt it. That's why movies are so powerful. They use technology to communicate, to keep an audience together and focused.

The "Yes We Can" video helped communicate Obama's essential optimism to the mass audience. By creating the video, we contributed to a national conversation and gave people a tool to express how they were feeling.

The most important thing about communicating is to check your ego at the door. Just listen hard to the message and don't try to take your ideas and stick it into their ideas. When communicating others' ideas, just give their voice, their concept, full expression. Beautiful things can happen.

4. Information should be universally available—but simultaneously protected.

One issue I'm really passionate about is making health information free of charge to anybody. I don't know if you've ever been sick, really sick, but if you go online to research your illness, it's hard to find anything legitimate. So I made a site, www.lybba.org, that helps patients on their journey. This site promotes the sharing of ideas between researchers and aims to make information available to all—patients, doctors, and researchers.

At the same time, we have to protect information. Right now, intellectual copyrights have no meaning on the Web. Copyrights today are undervalued, but some day I think copyrights will become valuable again. It will just take some time.

Consider Picasso. Today, his work doesn't have a place on the Web. His art is foddered around. It's not protected, and no one manages how it looks. And it's worse for Shakespeare and Edgar Allen Poe. Sure, "The Raven" is great, and it's impossible to destroy it, but I don't think that Poe would be looking at the shitty font someone uses to reprint it and think, "Oh, that's great."

155

// AS TOLD TO RAINN WILSON BY JESSE DYLAN, *filmmaker and founder of FreeForm, a media-driven company in the service of ideas that change culture*

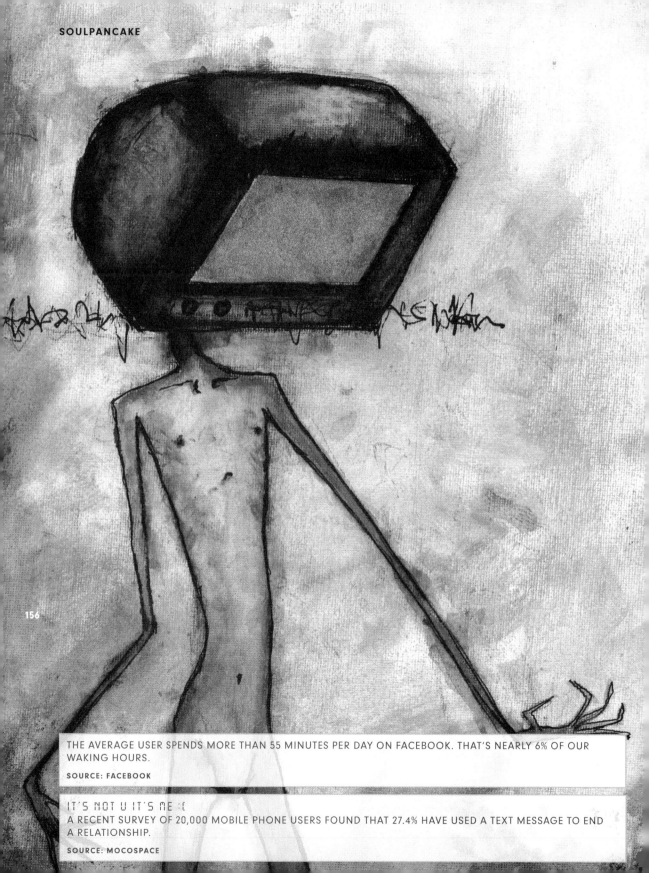

THE AVERAGE USER SPENDS MORE THAN 55 MINUTES PER DAY ON FACEBOOK. THAT'S NEARLY 6% OF OUR WAKING HOURS.

SOURCE: FACEBOOK

IT'S NOT U IT'S ME :(
A RECENT SURVEY OF 20,000 MOBILE PHONE USERS FOUND THAT 27.4% HAVE USED A TEXT MESSAGE TO END A RELATIONSHIP.

SOURCE: MOCOSPACE

"IT [THE RADIO] IS A MEDIUM OF ENTERTAINMENT WHICH PERMITS MILLIONS OF PEOPLE TO LISTEN TO THE SAME JOKE AT THE SAME TIME, AND YET REMAIN LONESOME." // **T.S. ELIOT**

"IF IT KEEPS UP, MAN WILL ATROPHY ALL HIS LIMBS BUT THE PUSH-BUTTON FINGER." // **FRANK LLOYD WRIGHT**

WHAT CAN TECHNOLOGY NEVER REPLACE?

DIG DEEPER

HOW HAS TECHNOLOGY AFFECTED YOUR RELATIONSHIPS?

WHAT TECHNOLOGIES HAVE HAD THE MOST POWERFUL IMPACT ON THE WORLD?

HOW CAN WE ENSURE TECHNOLOGY IS ONLY USED FOR GOOD?

AIRBRUSHED
AUTO-TUNED

LIST FIVE WAYS TECHNOLOGY ENHANCES ART
AND FIVE WAYS IT DESTROYS IT.

ENHANCES

DESTROYS

1.

1.

2.

2.

3.

3.

4.

4.

5.

5.

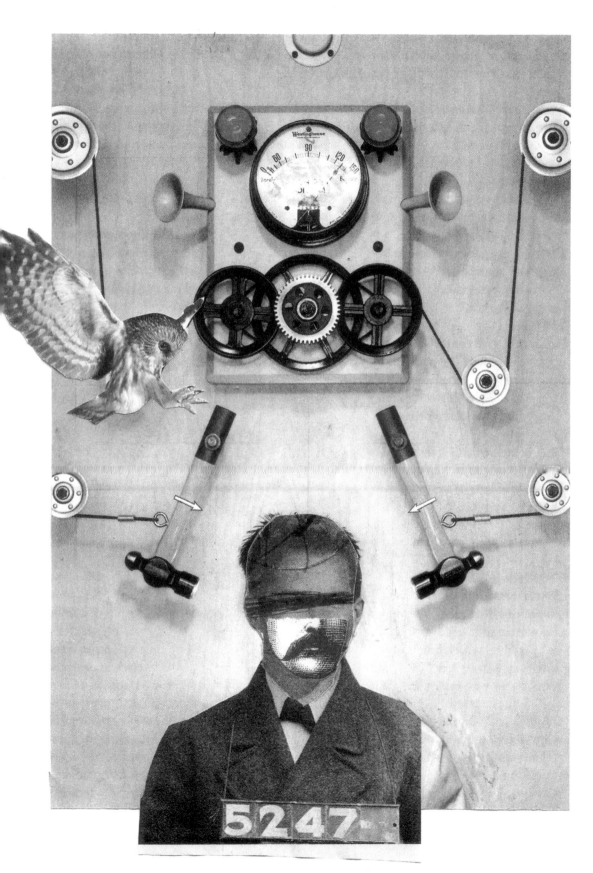

WITH $18,000 AND A LITTLE IN VITRO FERTILIZATION, A TECHNIQUE CALLED PRE-IMPLANTATION GENETIC DIAGNOSIS WILL ALLOW YOU TO CHOOSE THE GENDER OF YOUR CHILD.

SOURCE: CNN

WHO NEEDS CONDOMS WHEN YOU'VE GOT CORN? ACCORDING TO A STUDY AT THE UNIVERSITY OF VIENNA, MICE THAT WERE FED A PARTICULAR STRAIN OF GENETICALLY MODIFIED CORN OVER A PERIOD OF 20 WEEKS SHOWED A STATISTICALLY SIGNIFICANT DECREASE IN FERTILITY.

SOURCE: GREENPEACE

HOW SHOULD SCIENCE PROCEED WITH GENETIC ENGINEERING?

"HUMANS HAVE LONG SINCE POSSESSED THE TOOLS FOR CRAFTING A BETTER WORLD. WHERE LOVE, COMPASSION, ALTRUISM, AND JUSTICE HAVE FAILED, GENETIC MANIPULATION WILL NOT SUCCEED." // **GINA MARANTO**

"WE HAVE GREAT RESPECT FOR THE HUMAN SPECIES. WE LIKE EACH OTHER. WE'D LIKE TO BE BETTER... BUT EVOLUTION CAN BE JUST DAMN CRUEL, AND TO SAY THAT WE'VE GOT A PERFECT GENOME AND THERE'S SOME SANCTITY TO IT... IT'S UTTER SILLINESS. AND THE OTHER THING, BECAUSE NO ONE REALLY HAS THE GUTS TO SAY IT: I MEAN, IF WE COULD MAKE BETTER HUMAN BEINGS BY KNOWING HOW TO ADD GENES, WHY SHOULDN'T WE DO IT?" // **JAMES WATSON**

161

DIG
DEEPER WHAT WOULD YOU CHANGE ABOUT YOUR DNA?   SHOULD WE CLONE HUMAN BEINGS?
IS GENETIC ENGINEERING STEPPING ON GOD'S TOES?

"MAN IS THE ONLY ANIMAL FOR WHOM HIS OWN EXISTENCE IS A PROBLEM WHICH HE HAS TO SOLVE." // **ERICH FROMM**

162

RESEARCH AT BOWLING GREEN STATE UNIVERSITY SUGGESTS THAT HUMAN LAUGHTER HAS ROBUST ROOTS IN OUR ANIMALIAN PAST. THE STUDY OBSERVED RATS AND FOUND THAT WHEN THEY "PLAY," THEY OFTEN CHIRP—A PRIMITIVE FORM OF LAUGHTER.

SOURCE: *National Geographic*

"WE ARE JUST AN ADVANCED BREED OF MONKEYS ON A MINOR PLANET OF A VERY AVERAGE STAR. BUT WE CAN UNDERSTAND THE UNIVERSE. THAT MAKES US SOMETHING VERY SPECIAL." // **STEPHEN HAWKING**

WHAT'S THE DIFFERENCE BETWEEN HUMANS AND ANIMALS?

THE MEDIAN NUMBER OF LIFETIME FEMALE SEXUAL PARTNERS FOR MEN IS SEVEN; THE MEDIAN NUMBER OF LIFETIME MALE SEXUAL PARTNERS FOR WOMEN IS FOUR. THE GRAY WOLF TENDS TO MATE FOR LIFE.

SOURCE: NATIONAL CENTER FOR HEALTH STATISTICS; DAVIDSON COLLEGE

DIG DEEPER

WHAT CAN WE LEARN FROM ANIMALS?

SHOULD HUMAN RIGHTS SUPERSEDE THE RIGHTS OF ANIMALS?

DO ANIMALS KNOW RIGHT FROM WRONG?

GYRATE YOUR GENIUS

"WHERE A NEW INVENTION PROMISES TO BE USEFUL, IT OUGHT TO BE TRIED." // THOMAS JEFFERSON

IF THE U.S. PATENT AND TRADEMARK OFFICE CAN SIGN OFF ON CHIA PETS AND THE BEERBRELLA, THEN WHAT'S STOPPING YOU FROM THROWING YOUR IDEA INTO THE MIX?

STEP 1 THINK OF A PROBLEM THAT IRRITATES YOU.

STEP 2 CHANNEL YOUR INNER INVENTOR.

STEP 3 CREATE A SOLUTION. NO MATTER HOW FAR-FETCHED IT SEEMS, SKETCH IT OUT AND NAME IT.

164

NAME YOUR INVENTION

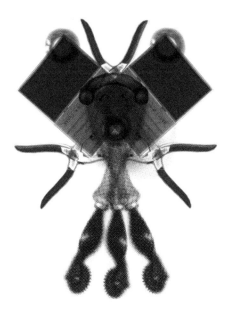

{ OBJ # ONE }

it can store – pinch – perforate

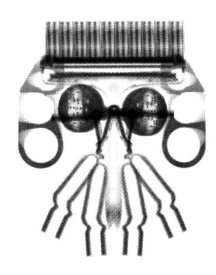

{ OBJ # FOUR }

it can tune – measure – heat
shave – tape

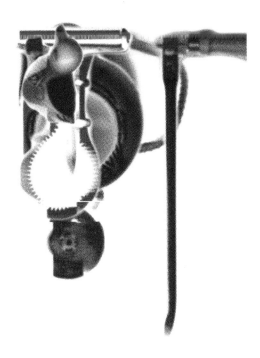

{ OBJ # FIVE }

it can saw – open – peel
contain – pour – quack

{ OBJ # NINE }

it can massage – open – saw
slip – see

165

MILLIONS PRAY WHEN THEY ARE ILL OR KNOW SOMEONE WHO IS. BUT RESEARCH SUGGESTS THAT THE PRAYERS MAY NOT IMPROVE A PATIENT'S RECOVERY. IN A STUDY OF 700 HEART PATIENTS, CARDIOLOGISTS AT DUKE UNIVERSITY SHOWED THAT THOSE WHO HAD PEOPLE PRAYING FOR THEM FROM A DISTANCE, AND WITHOUT THEIR KNOWLEDGE, WERE NO LESS LIKELY TO SUFFER A MAJOR COMPLICATION, END UP BACK IN THE HOSPITAL, OR DIE.

SOURCE: *Washington Post*

THE PLACEBO EFFECT IS SOMEHOW GETTING STRONGER. FROM 2001 TO 2008, IT'S ESTIMATED THAT THE SO-CALLED EFFECT SIZE (A MEASURE OF STATISTICAL SIGNIFICANCE) IN PLACEBO GROUPS HAD NEARLY DOUBLED. TRANSLATION: SUGAR PILLS ARE GIVING MEDICATIONS A RUN FOR THEIR MONEY.

SOURCE: *Wired*

HOW DO OUR MINDS AFFECT OUR HEALTH?

DIG
DEEPER

WHAT DO YOU NEED TO FEEL PHYSICALLY HEALTHY?
WHAT DO YOU NEED TO FEEL MENTALLY HEALTHY?
WHAT DO YOU NEED TO FEEL SPIRITUALLY HEALTHY?

"DISEASES OF THE SOUL ARE MORE DANGEROUS AND MORE NUMEROUS THAN THOSE OF THE BODY." // CICERO

"THE FACT THAT THE MIND RULES THE BODY IS, IN SPITE OF ITS NEGLECT BY BIOLOGY AND MEDICINE, THE MOST FUNDAMENTAL FACT WHICH WE KNOW ABOUT THE PROCESS OF LIFE." // **DR. FRANZ ALEXANDER**

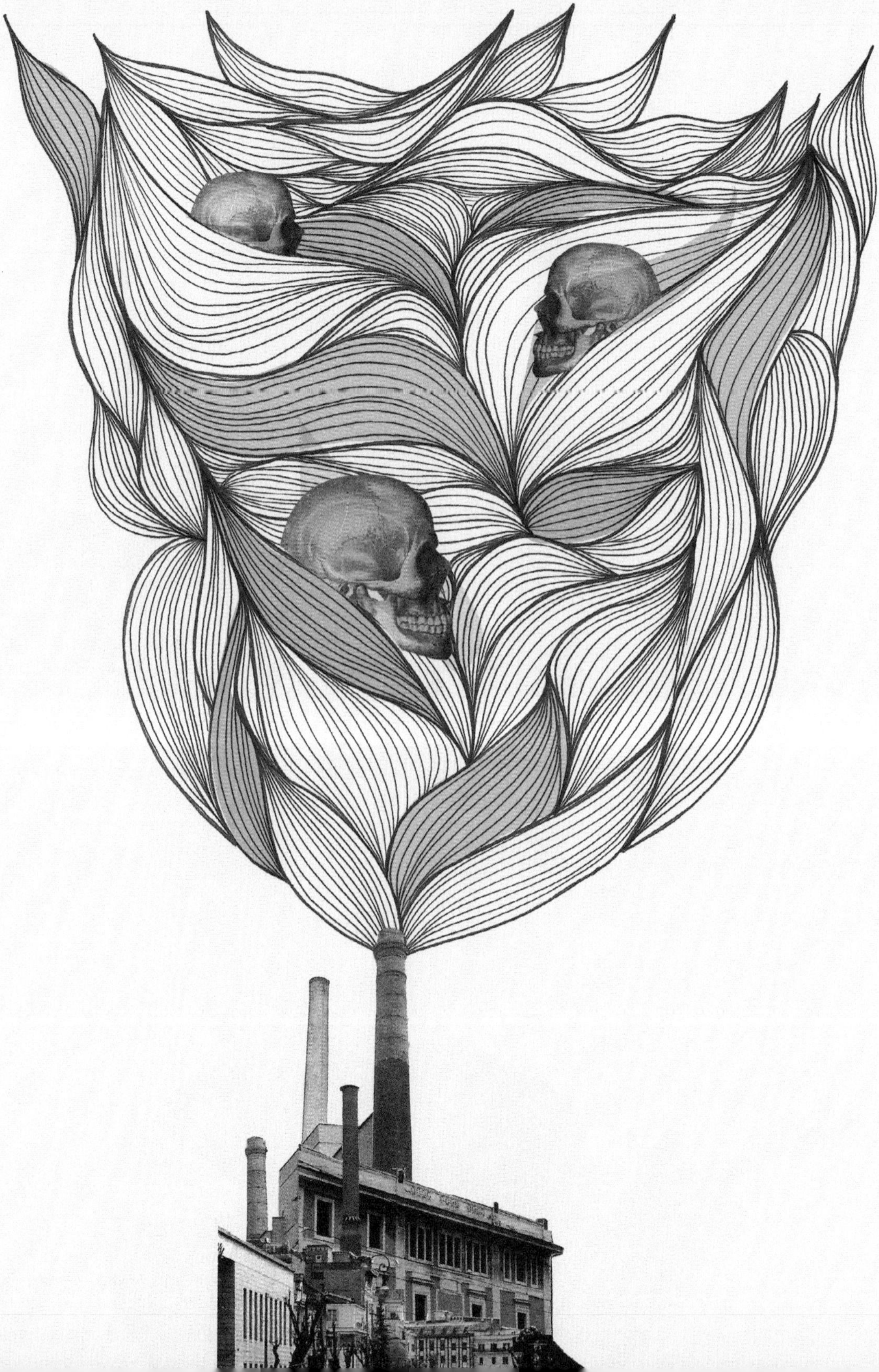

"THIS IS A BEAUTIFUL PLANET AND NOT AT ALL FRAGILE. EARTH CAN WITHSTAND SIGNIFICANT VOLCANIC ERUPTIONS, TECTONIC CATACLYSMS, AND ICE AGES. BUT THIS CANNY, INTELLIGENT, PROLIFIC, AND EXTREMELY SELF-CENTERED HUMAN CREATURE HAD PROVEN HIMSELF CAPABLE OF MORE DESTRUCTION OF LIFE THAN MOTHER NATURE HERSELF... WE'VE GOT TO BE STOPPED." // **MICHAEL L. FISCHER**

"SOON SILENCE WILL HAVE PASSED INTO LEGEND. MAN HAS TURNED HIS BACK ON SILENCE. DAY AFTER DAY HE INVENTS MACHINES AND DEVICES THAT INCREASE NOISE AND DISTRACT HUMANITY FROM THE ESSENCE OF LIFE, CONTEMPLATION, MEDITATION... TOOTING, HOWLING, SCREECHING, BOOMING, CRASHING, WHISTLING, GRINDING, AND TRILLING BOLSTER HIS EGO. HIS ANXIETY SUBSIDES. HIS INHUMAN VOID SPREADS MONSTROUSLY LIKE A GRAY VEGETATION." // **JEAN ARP**

HOW ARE YOU HARMING THE PLANET?

169

A RECENT STUDY FOUND THAT THE U.S. AIRLINE INDUSTRY DISCARDS ENOUGH ALUMINUM CANS IN A YEAR TO BUILD 58 BOEING 747 AIRPLANES.

SOURCE: NATURAL RESOURCES DEFENSE COUNCIL

ONE OF THE MAJOR CONSEQUENCES OF LIGHT POLLUTION IS THAT ONLY 3% OF STARS CAN BE SEEN TODAY FROM MOST CITIES AND SUBURBS. ONE MUST TRAVEL SEVERAL HUNDREDS OF MILES FROM AN URBAN CENTER TO WITNESS A CLEAR, STARRY SKY.

SOURCE: INTERNATIONAL DARK-SKY ASSOCIATION

DIG DEEPER

WHAT DO YOU DO TO HELP THE ENVIRONMENT?
WHAT IS YOUR BIGGEST FEAR FOR THE EARTH?
HOW ARE YOU A CONSCIENTIOUS CONSUMER?

Paper Repayment

Plant a tree for purchasing this book.

"TECHNOLOGY... THE KNACK OF SO ARRANGING THE WORLD THAT WE DON'T HAVE TO EXPERIENCE IT." // **MAX FRISCH**

TECH DETOX

TAKE A DAY AND COMPLETELY UNPLUG. TURN OFF THE DEVICES THAT COMPETE FOR YOUR ATTENTION. EXPLORE THE WORLD THAT EXISTS WITHOUT YOU TURNING IT ON.

173

PROGRESS

PRO·GRESS |ˈpragrəs | noun

1. **a)** a royal journey marked by pomp and pageant
   b) a state procession
   c) a tour or circuit made by an official (as a judge)
   d) an expedition, journey, or march through a region
2. a forward or onward movement (as to an objective or to a goal); advance
3. gradual betterment; especially, the progressive development of humankind

SYNONYMS
ADVANCE,
AMELIORATION,
ANABASIS,
BETTERMENT,
BOOST, BREAK,
BREAKTHROUGH,
BUILDUP, COURSE,
DASH, DEVELOPMENT,
EVOLUTION,
EVOLVEMENT,
EXPEDITION,
FLOWERING,
GROWTH, HEADWAY,
HIKE, IMPETUS,
IMPROVEMENT,
INCREASE, JOURNEY,
LUNGE, MARCH,
MOMENTUM,
MOTION, MOVEMENT,
ONGOING, PACE,
PASSAGE, PROCESS,
PROCESSION,
PROFICIENCY,
PROGRESSION,
PROMOTION, RATE,
RISE, STEP FORWARD,
STRIDE, TOUR,
UNFOLDING,
VOYAGE, WAY

"PROGRESS IS MAN'S ABILITY TO COMPLICATE SIMPLICITY." // THOR HEYERDAHL

"WE ALL WANT PROGRESS, BUT IF YOU'RE ON THE WRONG ROAD, PROGRESS MEANS DOING AN ABOUT-TURN AND WALKING BACK TO THE RIGHT ROAD; IN THAT CASE, THE MAN WHO TURNS BACK SOONEST IS THE MOST PROGRESSIVE." // C. S. LEWIS

"GOD LOVED THE BIRDS AND INVENTED TREES. MAN LOVED THE BIRDS AND INVENTED CAGES."
// JACQUES DEVAL

174   "Understand that most problems are a good sign. Problems indicate that progress is being made, wheels are turning, you are moving toward your goals. Beware when you have no problems. Then you've really got a problem... problems are like landmarks of progress." // SCOTT ALEXANDER

"THE TEST OF OUR PROGRESS IS NOT WHETHER WE ADD TO THE ABUNDANCE OF THOSE WHO HAVE MUCH, IT IS WHETHER WE PROVIDE ENOUGH TO THOSE WHO HAVE LITTLE." // FRANKLIN D. ROOSEVELT

YOU RE-DEFINE

PROGRESS IS

PROGRESS ISN'T

LIFE, DEATH & LIVING

LEGACY
CHILDHOOD
SERVICE
ACTIVISM
FEAR OF DEATH
PRIORITIES
LIFE AFTER DEATH
PURPOSE
FEELING ALIVE
WHAT IS SUCCESS?

WILD GOOSE

All that I've learned
Is sometimes wells run dry
It don't matter the hour or the season

Gone gone gone is your wild goose
And it never leaves giving a reason

When you're up, you'll be up
You'll have love, you'll have luck
And when it goes, you won't see it coming

And gone gone gone you'll be hearing that song
As it floats back to you down the North wind

Oh what kind of law draws the apples to the ground?
And what kind of love draws the orbits?
And where, oh where, went your wild goose?
And what made you once think you could hold it?

**// LYRICS WRITTEN EXCLUSIVELY FOR SOULPANCAKE
BY JOSH RITTER,** *American musician*

LISTEN UP: Hear Josh Ritter's "Wild Goose" at
www.soulpancakebook.com.

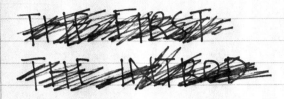

THE STARTING LINE

SOME OF THE BEST AUTOBIOGRAPHIES
BEGIN WITH AN INTENSE TURNING
POINT IN AN EXTRAORDINARY LIFE.

x x x x x x x x x

"My father always said I would do something
big one day.

'I've got a feeling about you, John Osbourne,'
he'd tell me, after he'd had a few beers.
'You're either going to do something very special,
or you're going to go to prison.'

And he was right, my old man.

I was in prison before my eighteenth birthday."

// Opening lines from "I Am Ozzy" by Ozzy Osbourne
(Grand Central Publishing, 2010)

x x x x x x x x x

WHAT WOULD YOU WANT YOUR OPENING LINES TO BE?

xxxxxxxx

xxxxxxxxx

THERE'S ALWAYS TIME TO BUILD A FORT

List five things you can learn from a 5-year-old.

01

02

03

04

05

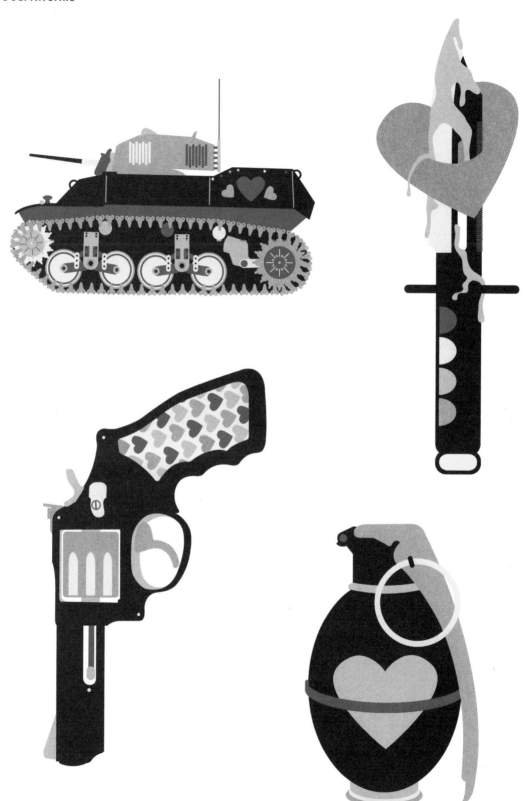

IN THE UNITED KINGDOM, COMMUNITY SERVICE, ALSO CALLED "COMPULSORY UNPAID WORK," IS REQUIRED PRIOR TO GRADUATING HIGH SCHOOL.

SOURCE: *New York Daily News*

PRIVATE AND VOLUNTARY ORGANIZATIONS, TOGETHER WITH RELIGIOUS ORGANIZATIONS AND VOLUNTEERS, GIVE MORE IN AID TO DEVELOPING COUNTRIES THAN THE U.S. GOVERNMENT DOES. IN 2007, U.S. PRIVATE PHILANTHROPY TOTALED $36.9 BILLION, MORE THAN 1.5 TIMES GOVERNMENT AID FOR THE SAME PERIOD.

SOURCE: *The 2009 Index of Global Philanthropy and Remittances*

WHAT CAN YOU DO TO MAKE THIS WORLD A LITTLE LESS SCREWED UP?

DIG DEEPER

WHO HAS HELPED MAKE YOUR LIFE A LITTLE LESS SCREWED UP?

SHOULD COMMUNITY SERVICE BE MANDATORY?

WHEN IT COMES TO VOLUNTEER WORK, WHAT STOPS YOU FROM STEPPING UP?

"ONE OF THE SECRETS OF LIFE IS THAT ALL THAT IS REALLY WORTH THE DOING IS WHAT WE DO FOR OTHERS." // **LEWIS CARROLL**

"BE CAREFUL TO AVOID INGESTING TOXINS IN THE FORM OF VIOLENT TV PROGRAMS, VIDEO GAMES, MOVIES, MAGAZINES, AND BOOKS. WHEN WE WATCH THAT KIND OF VIOLENCE, WE WATER OUR OWN NEGATIVE SEEDS... AND EVENTUALLY WE WILL THINK AND ACT OUT OF THOSE SEEDS." // **THICH NHAT HANH**

184

In the 1960s, more than 200,000 people marched on Washington, D.C., to rally for civil rights. In 1999, thousands of people protested the World Trade Organization's corporate trade negotiations. In the United States, when we rally, we rally big. But maybe the impact can be just as great on a smaller scale.

STEP 1
Find a couple of little people. Try LEGO figures, G.I. Joes, or Barbie dolls.

STEP 2
Emblazon a tiny piece of paper with something you stand for.

STEP 3
Stage your protest in a public space.

STEP 4
Walk away and let the world hear your battle cry... or should we say whisper?

185

// PATRICK STUMP

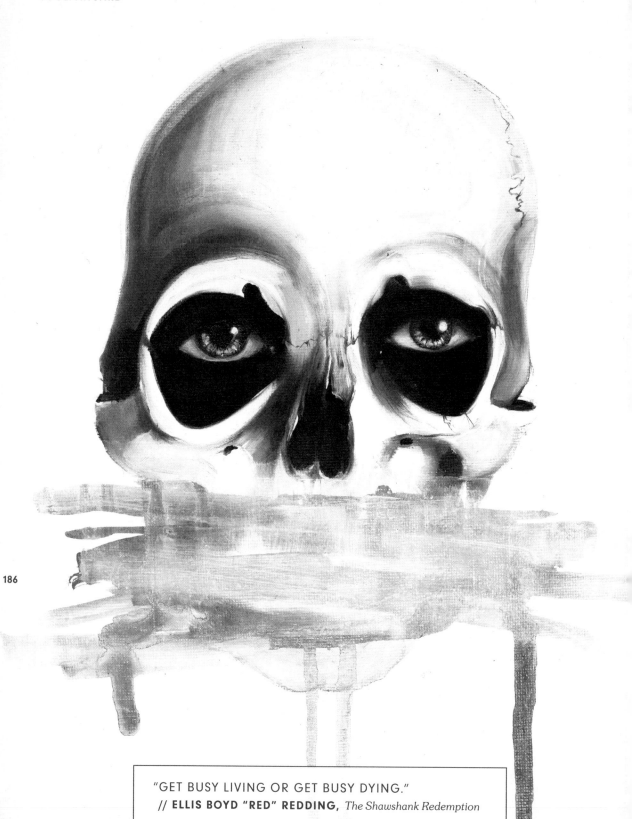

186

"GET BUSY LIVING OR GET BUSY DYING."
// **ELLIS BOYD "RED" REDDING,** *The Shawshank Redemption*

"IT BEGAN IN MYSTERY, AND IT WILL END IN MYSTERY, BUT WHAT A SAVAGE AND BEAUTIFUL LIFE LIES IN BETWEEN." // **DIANE ACKERMAN**

WOULD YOU WANT TO KNOW THE EXACT MOMENT YOU ARE GOING TO DIE?

187

DIG DEEPER

WOULD YOU WANT TO KNOW THE EXACT MOMENT THE PERSON YOU CARE MOST ABOUT WILL DIE?
WHAT THINGS IN LIFE SHOULD ALWAYS REMAIN A MYSTERY?
WHEN THE TIME COMES, HOW DO YOU WANT TO GO?

IN THE MINUTE IT'S TAKEN YOU TO READ THIS PAGE,

108 **PEOPLE AROUND THE WORLD HAVE DIED.**
SOURCE: CIA *World Factbook*

ON AVERAGE, 100 PEOPLE IN THE UNITED STATES CHOKE TO DEATH ON BALLPOINT PENS EVERY YEAR.
SOURCE: CENTERS FOR DISEASE CONTROL AND PREVENTION

 *vs* **134**

THE MOST ORGASMS RECORDED IN ONE HOUR FOR A MAN IS 16.
THE MOST ORGASMS RECORDED IN ONE HOUR FOR A WOMAN IS 134.

SOURCE: *Men's Health*

IF YOU ONLY HAD ONE HOUR LEFT TO LIVE, HOW WOULD YOU SPEND IT?

188

 DIG DEEPER

WHAT ONE EXPERIENCE ARE *YOU* MOST GLAD TO HAVE HAD?
WHAT'S YOUR BIGGEST REGRET ABOUT THE LIFE YOU'VE LIVED TO DATE?
WHOSE LEGACY DO YOU MOST REVERE?

AMONG ANIMALS, THE GIANT TORTOISE LIVES ONE OF THE LONGEST
LIVES, ABOUT 177 YEARS IN CAPTIVITY. THE MAYFLY, MEANWHILE, LIVES
THE SHORTEST—BETWEEN HALF AN HOUR AND 24 HOURS.

SOURCE: *Encyclopedia Britannica*

"SINCE TIME IS THE ONE IMMATERIAL OBJECT WHICH WE CANNOT INFLUENCE—NEITHER SPEED UP NOR SLOW DOWN, ADD TO NOR DIMINISH—IT IS AN IMPONDERABLY VALUABLE GIFT." // **MAYA ANGELOU**

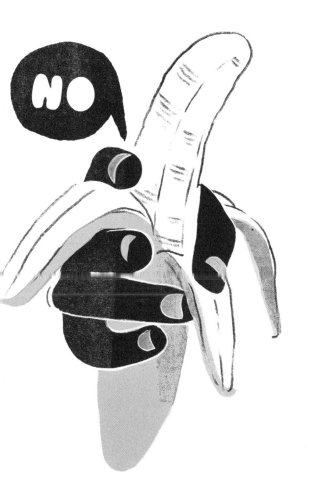

189

"TIME YOU ENJOYED WASTING IS NOT WASTED TIME." // **BERTRAND RUSSELL**

NEARLY 800 NEAR-DEATH EXPERIENCES HAPPEN EVERY DAY IN THE UNITED STATES.

SOURCE: NEAR DEATH EXPERIENCE RESEARCH FOUNDATION

THE NUMBER OF CREMATIONS IN THE UNITED STATES IS FORECAST TO DOUBLE TO ABOUT HALF OF ALL DEATHS BY 2020.

SOURCE: *St. Petersburg Times*

"DEATH IS NO MORE THAN PASSING FROM ONE ROOM INTO ANOTHER. BUT THERE'S A DIFFERENCE FOR ME, YOU KNOW. BECAUSE IN THAT OTHER ROOM I SHALL BE ABLE TO SEE." // **HELEN KELLER**

What do you hope happens when you die?

DIG DEEPER

WHY ARE WE SO AFRAID OF DEATH?

WHAT ONE QUESTION WOULD YOU WANT TO ASK A PERSON WHO RECENTLY DIED?

IF THERE'S NO LIFE AFTER DEATH, DO YOU WANT TO LIVE FOREVER?

"FROM MY ROTTING BODY, FLOWERS SHALL GROW AND I AM IN THEM AND THAT IS ETERNITY." // **EDVARD MUNCH**

"FOCUSING YOUR LIFE SOLELY ON MAKING A BUCK SHOWS A POVERTY OF AMBITION. IT ASKS TOO LITTLE OF YOURSELF. AND IT WILL LEAVE YOU UNFULFILLED." // **BARACK OBAMA**

WHAT IS TH
OF YOUR L

 DIG DEEPER

DOES YOUR SENSE OF PURPOSE EVOLVE?
IF YOU LAND YOUR IDEAL JOB, HAVE YOU ACHIEVED YOUR PURPOSE?
WHO HAS MOST INFLUENCED YOUR LIFE'S PURPOSE?

"OUR SOULS ARE HUNGRY FOR MEANING, FOR THE SENSE THAT WE HAVE FIGURED OUT HOW TO LIVE SO THAT OUR LIVES MATTER, SO THAT THE WORLD WILL BE AT LEAST A LITTLE BIT DIFFERENT FOR OUR HAVING PASSED THROUGH IT." // **RABBI HAROLD KUSHNER**

E PURPOSE

E?

193

THE AVERAGE U.S. WORKER WILL HAVE 15 DIFFERENT JOBS SPANNING UP TO FIVE DIFFERENT CAREERS OVER THE COURSE OF HIS OR HER LIFETIME.

SOURCE: U.S. DEPARTMENT OF LABOR

RICK WARREN'S *The Purpose Driven Life* HAS MORE THAN 30 MILLION COPIES IN PRINT AND IS ONE OF THE BEST-SELLING NONFICTION BOOKS OF ALL TIME.

SOURCE: *Publishers Weekly*

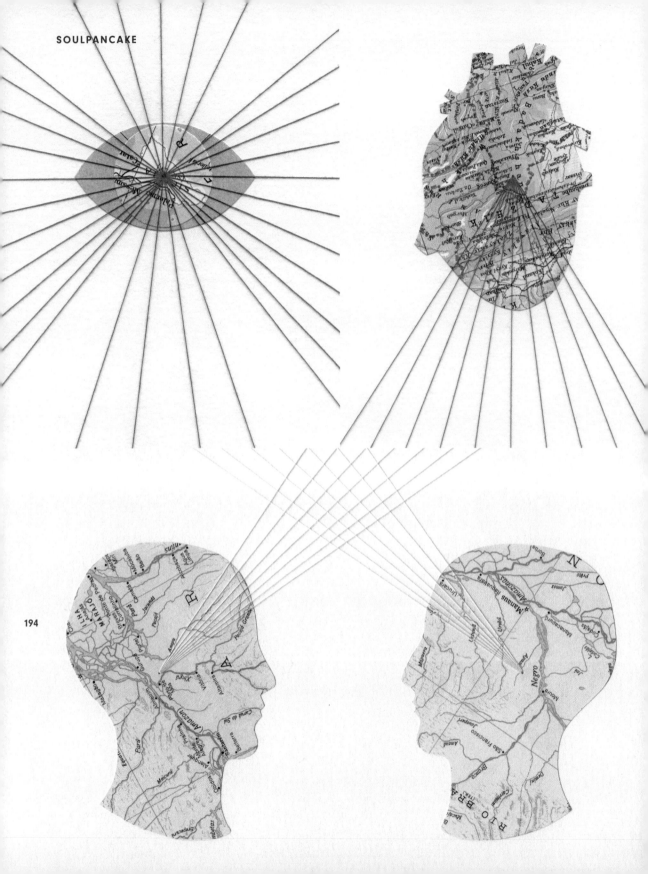

LIVE A LITTLE

Good news—if you're reading this book, you're alive. But just how alive? Have you really lived if you haven't faced a full spectrum of experiences? Here are 52 ways for you to live a little more. Tackle one a week for a year.

- ❏ Get punched.
- ❏ Tell a friend a truth they don't want to hear.
  (This might help you achieve the first item on the list.)
- ❏ Burn a book you hated.
- ❏ Eat something that challenges your gag reflexes.
- ❏ Jump on a bus without knowing the end destination.
- ❏ Grow something.
- ❏ Walk barefoot all day.
- ❏ Hit something hard enough to break it.
- ❏ Stand on the edge of a rooftop.
- ❏ Stay up all night.
- ❏ Don't get out of bed for an entire day.
- ❏ Read a book cover-to-cover without stopping.
- ❏ Feed yourself for a week with only $7.
- ❏ Plunge your hands in soil.
- ❏ Take a nap on a park bench.
- ❏ Stand in the pouring rain. Get drenched.
- ❏ Spend a day with the oldest person you know.
- ❏ Go to the concert of a band you've never heard of.
- ❏ Don't use utensils to eat all day.
- ❏ Shower in the dark.
- ❏ Take your neighbor a cup of coffee.
- ❏ Climb a tree.
- ❏ Feed a stray dog or cat.
- ❏ Double-tip your server.
- ❏ Read a book that makes your brain hurt.
- ❏ Give a stranger a sincere compliment.
- ❏ Skip, don't walk.

- ❏ Grab some friends and start a pillow fight in a public place.
- ❏ Don't wear underwear.
- ❏ Trade lunches with somebody.
- ❏ Perfect your signature.
- ❏ Scream at the top of your lungs in the middle of a park.
- ❏ Buy and play a harmonica.
- ❏ Pretend to know a stranger.
- ❏ Go to a thrift store and buy an entire outfit. Wear it the rest of the day.
- ❏ Watch one of your parents' favorite movies.
- ❏ Get a knife. Get a stick. Whittle something.
- ❏ Make a meal out of whatever you have in your fridge.
- ❏ Write your will.
- ❏ Leave flowers at a random doorstep.
- ❏ Pick up every piece of trash you see today.
- ❏ Next time you get into an argument, let the other person win.
- ❏ Create art with a kid. Embrace the mess.
- ❏ Memorize a poem.
- ❏ Draw something in the steam on the mirror after your next shower.
- ❏ Have a conversation with a homeless person.
- ❏ Buy an album based solely on its cover art.
- ❏ Don't use the words "Yes" or "No" for a day.
- ❏ Shoot a rifle at a firing range.
- ❏ Cut your own hair.
- ❏ Bribe someone.
- ❏ Hold your breath for as long as you can.

SUCCESS

THEY DEFINE

SUC·CESS | sək'ses| noun

1. outcome, result
2. a) degree or measure of succeeding;
   b) favorable or desired outcome; also the attainment of wealth, favor, or eminence;
3. one that succeeds

"You know you are on the road to success if you would do your job and not be paid for it." // OPRAH WINFREY

"TO LAUGH OFTEN AND MUCH; TO WIN THE RESPECT OF INTELLIGENT PEOPLE AND THE AFFECTION OF CHILDREN ... TO LEAVE THE WORLD A BETTER PLACE ... TO KNOW EVEN ONE LIFE HAS BREATHED EASIER BECAUSE YOU HAVE LIVED. THIS IS TO HAVE SUCCEEDED."
// RALPH WALDO EMERSON

"SUCCESS IS

99%

FAILURE."

// SOICHIRO HONDA

SYNONYMS
ACCOMPLISHMENT, ACHIEVEMENT, ADVANCE, ARRIVAL, ASCENDANCY, ATTAINMENT, BED OF ROSES, BENEFIT, BIG HIT, BOOM, CLOVER, CONSUMMATION, DO WELL, ÉCLAT, EMINENCE, FAME, FLYING COLORS, FORTUNE, FRUITION, GAIN, GOOD LUCK, GOOD TIMES, GRAND SLAM, GRAVY TRAIN, HAPPINESS, HAPPY DAYS, HIT, KILLING, LAP OF LUXURY, LAUGHTER, MATURATION, PROFIT, PROGRESS, PROSPERITY, REALIZATION, REWARD, SAVVY, SENSATION, SNAP, STRIKE, SUCCESSFULNESS, TRIUMPH, VICTORY, WALKAWAY, WALKOVER, WIN

196

"YOU KNOW, THE FINEST LINE A MAN WILL WALK IS BETWEEN SUCCESS AT WORK AND SUCCESS AT HOME." // **DEL GRIFFITH**, *Planes, Trains & Automobiles*

"The distance between insanity and genius is measured only by success."

// **ELLIOT CARVER**, *Tomorrow Never Dies*

YOU RE-DEFINE

SUCCESS IS

SUCCESS ISN'T

Devon Gundry

01 I'm grateful that I slacked off in my sixth-grade computer class, since typing with all of the wrong fingers naturally holds my hands in a position that prevents carpal tunnel syndrome.

02 Depending on when you met me, I might have been: a checkers champion, the kid who squirted Super Glue in his eye, a competitive Ping-Pong player, Tweedle Dum, a high school valedictorian, a fake blond, $\frac{1}{12}$ of an all-male a capella group, a graduate of the Vanderbilt School of Engineering, a nomad, a street musician, or a pigeon assassin.

03 My little brother is smarter than me. My little sister is a better writer than I'll ever be. My mom has twice as much energy as me. And my dad's mustache makes mine look like a wannabe.

04 Somehow, I convinced one of my co-authors to marry me. Now I have a wife. And she's so dang cool.

05 I co-created SoulPancake to see what happens when you simultaneously smash art and spirituality into your brain stem.

Golriz Lucina

01 I'm a Persian-Armenian-Kiwi-Australian who drinks copious amounts of Earl Grey tea and laments the use of Comic Sans font.

02 When I was a toddler, I supposedly walked around with a pen and paper "taking notes." This makes me two things: a nerd from a young age, and someone destined to get a master's degree in publishing.

03 My family members could not be more different from one another. The mix includes one rocket scientist brother; one fashionista sister; one honey-harvesting, lover-of-all-creatures-big-and-small mother; and one classical music enthusiast father. And then there's me—a camera junkie and jetsetter with a penchant for tasty type treatments (and alliteration).

04 I have a big crush on one of my co-authors.

05 I believe that questions are often more essential than answers. And that is why I love creating content for SoulPancake.

Shabnam Mogharabi

01 I have been told repeatedly that Monica from *Friends* is my alter-ego—a super-competitive neat freak who loves to cook and has slightly unruly hair.

02 I was far too well-read as a kid, using words like "legumes" and "atrocious" before I was 10. I still love language and try to learn a few phrases for every country I visit. Chinese was the most difficult. *Wǒ shì miguórén* took forever to master.

03 I once wrote an article about the high drowning rates of minorities. The story later hit the *New York Times*, inspired a movie (*Pride*), and the Red Cross launched an inner-city learn-to-swim campaign. That one story showed me the power of change. It's also why I love being a journalist.

04 My family is truly funny in Farsi. My five loud, crazy younger siblings are my best friends. And my parents live *right* next door to my grandparents, which means every day with them is like *Everybody Loves Raymond* meets *My Big, Fat Greek Wedding*.

05 I believe in hard work, integrity, and that each person must define his or her own philosophy on life. And that is why I love the mission of SoulPancake.

Rainn Wilson

01 At one point in high school, I was on the chess team, marching band, computer club, debate club, pottery club, and Model United Nations. Now I am an actor.

02 Dear Reader: Please fill in what you'd like to see in my bio.

---

03 When I was 24, I got what is called a hydrocele in my left scrotum. The membrane that controls the flow of fluid was faulty, and my scrotum began to fill, ever so slowly, with water until my ball was approximately the size of a mandarin orange. It's all better now.

04 "It is difficult / to get the news from poems / yet men die miserably every day / for lack / of what is found there." // **WILLIAM CARLOS WILLIAMS**

05 I co-created SoulPancake and my son, Walter.

199

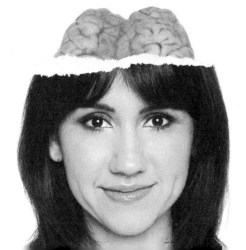
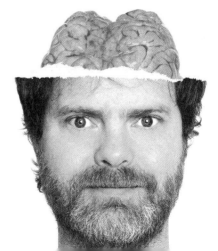

THE DESIGNERS

CHAHN CHUNG
Los Angeles, CA, USA
www.chahnchung.com

KAPONO CHUNG
New York, NY, USA
www.kaponochung.com

THE ARTISTS

MIKE MITCHELL
Los Angeles, CA, USA
www.sirmikeofmitchell.com
PG. I, II, 206

ROBYN CRAXTON
Dalton, NH, USA
www.robyncraxton.com
PG. 8-9

NICK SHEEHY
Leigh on Sea, England, UK
www.showchicken.com
PG. 2-3

MATT LYON
London, UK
www.c8six.com
PG. 10-11

SIGI KOLBE
Windhoek, Namibia
www.sigis-art.com
PG. 4-5

NICK TONGE
Manchester, England, UK
www.woomcreative.com
PG. 12-13

FIONA WATSON
Glasgow, Scotland, UK
www.fionawatson.co.uk
PG. 4-5

JULIET SEALS
Nashville, TN, USA
www.julietseals.com
PG. 12-13

200

JOEP ROOSEN
Amsterdam, Netherlands
www.flickr.com/joeproosen
PG. 4-5

GOLRIZ LUCINA & DEVON GUNDRY
Manhattan, NY, USA
www.19rockets.com
PG. 12-13

LAURA L. BURLTON
Houston, TX, USA
www.lauraburltonphotography.com
PG. 4-5

FAMOUS WHEN DEAD
Stoke on Trent, England, UK
www.famouswhendead.com
PG. 14-15

LAITH MCGREGOR
Melbourne, Australia
PG. 6-7

STACEY REES
Victoria, Australia
wallnut.etsy.com
PG. 16-17

HOLLIE CHASTAIN
Chattanooga, TN, USA
www.holliechastain.com
PG. 18-19

BRIAN MARSHALL
Wilmington, DE, USA
www.adopt-a-bot.com
PG. 24-25

TREASURE FREY
Los Angeles, CA, USA
www.treasurefrey.com
PG. 26-27

MARIO HUGO
New York, NY, USA
www.mariohugo.com
PG. 28-29

BOMBO!
Lucca, Italy
www.bomboland.com
PG. 30-31

GOLRIZ LUCINA & DEVON GUNDRY
Nashville, TN, USA
www.19rockets.com
PG. 32-33

ZIEMOWIT MAJ
London, England, UK
www.flickr.com/ziemowit_maj
PG. 34-35

SUZI SADLER
Brookyn, NY, USA
www.suzisadler.com
PG. 36-37

DAVID "DEEF" JACOBS
Oss, Holland
www.flickr.com/fletch_85
PG. 38-39

RYAN LASH
Toronto, Canada
www.ryanlashphotography.com
PG. 38-39

GOLRIZ LUCINA & DEVON GUNDRY
Nashville, TN, USA
www.19rockets.com
PG. 38-39

KRISTAL RAELENE MELSON
Singapore
www.kristalmelson.com
PG. 40-41

BRANDI STRICKLAND
Charlotte, NC, USA
www.brandistrickland.com
PG. 46-47

VH MCKENZIE
New York, NY, USA
vhmckenzie.blogspot.com
PG. 48-49

MIKKO WALAMIES
Helsinki, Finland
vhmckenzie.blogspot.com
PG. 50-51

SARAH BREWINGTON
Lakeland, FL, USA
www.flickr.com/sarahbrewphotography
PG. 52-53

ANNE-JULIE AUBRY
Aigues-Mortes, France
www.annejulieaubry.com
PG. 54-55

JOANNE CRUICKSHANK
Aberdeenshire, Scotland, UK
www.flickr.com/haggischick
PG. 56-57

JACQUELINE KARI BOS
Portland, OR, USA
www.jacquelinekari.com
PG. 58-59

J.R. ORCI
Studio City, CA, USA
www.flickr.com/jrorci
PG. 60-61

PAT PERRY
Grand Rapids, MI, USA
www.patperry.net
PG. 62-63

GLAUCO LIMA
São Paulo, Brazil
www.robotactivate.com
PG. 68-69

PAVEL BOLO
Tel Aviv, Israel
www.pavelbolo.com
PG. 70-71

KEITH LEE
Los Angeles, CA, USA / Hong Kong
dekanimal.etsy.com
PG. 72-73

TRE' JACKSON
Katy, TX, USA
www.trejack.com
PG. 74-75

PAMELA KLAFFKE
Calgary, Alberta, Canada
www.pamelaklaffke.com
PG. 76-77

CARMEN GONZALEZ
Hoogeveen, Netherlands
www.carmengonzalez.org
PG. 78-79

GOLRIZ LUCINA & DEVON GUNDRY
Nashville, TN, USA
www.19rockets.com
PG. 78-79

KIM CHAU
Queens, NY, USA
kimmychau.tumblr.com
PG. 78-79

SARA TERESA
Leeds, England, UK
www.sarateresa.com
PG. 78-79

JULIA POTT
London, England, UK
www.juliapott.com
PG. 80-81

LUPEN GRAINNE
Sebastopol, CA, USA
honeytree.etsy.com
PG. 82-83

JEANNIE L. PASKE
Portland, OR, USA
www.obsoleteworld.com
PG. 84-85

ALMA ELAINE SHOAF
Gainesville, FL, USA
www.almaelaine.com
PG. 90-91

GOLRIZ LUCINA & DEVON GUNDRY
New York, NY, USA
www.19rockets.com
PG. 92-93

GA-YOUNG KIM
Gyeonggi-do, Korea
www.kimgayoung.net
PG. 94-95

DANIEL GAFANHOTO
Rio de Janeiro, Brazil
www.danielgafanhoto.com
PG. 96-97

GOLRIZ LUCINA & DEVON GUNDRY
Piha Beach, New Zealand
www.19rockets.com
PG. 98-99

PAUL ARMSTRONG
Cincinnati, OH, USA
www.wiseacrephoto.com
PG. 100-101

MARC JOHNS
Victoria, British Columbia, Canada
www.marcjohns.com
PG. 102-103

REBEKAH CONSTANCE GARIBAY
Norman, OK, USA
rebekaeonstamee.etsy.com
PG. 104-105

MAXIME FRANCOUT
Montréal, Québec, Canada
www.maxf.eu
PG. 106-107

MORGAN BLAIR
Brooklyn, NY, USA
www.morganblair.com
PG. 112-113

BETSY LAM
Chicago, IL, USA
www.magicalthinklet.com
PG. 114-115

ALISON SAMBORN
Ann Arbor, MI, USA
www.alisonclairephotography.com
PG. 116-117

KELSEY MELAMED
Fallston, MD, USA
www.flickr.com/yanks4life23519
PG. 116-117

TROY HOLDEN
San Francisco, CA USA
www.calibersf.com
PG. 116-117

THOMAS LOTTERMOSER
Bonn, Germany
www.manganite.net
PG. 116-117

PAULINA KANEVSKY
Tel Aviv, Israel
www.behance.net/PoMiKa
PG. 118-119

JACK TEAGLE
Newquay, England, UK
www.jackteagle.co.uk
PG. 120-121

ELENA KALIS
Ft. Lauderdale, FL, USA
www.elenakalisphoto.com
PG. 122-123

ANDRÉ METZGER
New York, NY, USA
www.andremetzger.com
PG. 124-125

GIZEM VURAL
Istanbul, Turkey
www.behance.net/gecesintisi
PG. 126-127

JULIAN CALLOS
Los Angeles, CA, USA
www.juliancallos.com
PG. 128-129

MEET THE COLLABORATORS

203

LIAM SMITH & EMERSON BOERGADINE
Los Angeles, CA, USA
www.emersonsphotography.com
PG. 134-135

DEANNA BURKE
Boston, MA, USA
fuzzlefire.deviantart.com
PG. 156-157

GABRIELLE MARIN
Montréal, Québec, Canada
www.flickr.com/elleir
PG. 136-137

LILLIANNA PEREIRA
Northampton, MA, USA
www.lilliannapereira.com
PG. 158-159

JON TURNER
Evesham, England, UK
www.thisisjonturner.com
PG. 138-139

JENS-PETER GIESEL
Baden-Württemberg, Germany
www.behance.net/JensGiesel
PG. 160-161

JULES JULIEN
Paris, France
www.julesjulien.com
PG. 140-141

ANTOINE MORRIS & DAVID LONG
Toronto/Vancouver, Canada
www.everydaydesign.ca
PG. 162-163

WILMER MURILLO
Tegucigalpa, Honduras
www.wilmermurillo.com
PG. 142-143

ALICE SCHWAB & DANIEL ROSSI
Eindhoven, Netherlands
www.thedrawingmachine.nl
PG. 164-165

CHRIS PELL
Brighton, England, UK
www.chrispell.co.uk
PG. 144-145

ANTHONY ZINONOS
Norwich, England, UK
www.anthonyzinonos.com
PG. 166-167

204

FELIX KLEE
Passau, Germany
felixklee.daportfolio.com
PG. 146-147

RACHEL WILSON
Rome, Italy
www.hellowilson.co.uk
PG. 168-169

NATSUKI OTANI
Ely, England, UK
www.natsukiotani.co.uk
PG. 148-149

BLAINE FONTANA
Portland, OR, USA
www.thefontanastudios.com
PG. 170-171

MATT DUFFIN
Nevada City, CA, USA
www.mattduffin.com
PG. 150-151

AARON NACE
Huntersville, NC, USA
www.aaron-nace.com
PG. 172-173

SHABNAM MOGHARABI & CHRIS WOOD
San Francisco, CA, USA
www.shabnammogharabi.com
PG. 180-181

PATRICK WEBER
Nashville, TN, USA
www.societystyle.com
PG. 182-183

SHAHRIAR ASDOLLAH-ZADEH
Auckland, New Zealand
www.worldartcollective.org
PG. 184-185

JUSTIN WILLIAMS
Melbourne, Australia
www.justinleewilliams.net
PG. 186-187

GRANT COGHILL
Saalfelden, Austria
www.grantcoghill.com
PG. 188-189

GAVIN WORTH
San Francisco, CA, USA
www.gavinworth.com
PG. 190-191

JAUME OSMAN GRANDA
Barcelona, Spain
www.osmangranda.com
PG. 192-193

SHANNON RANKIN
Rangeley, ME, USA
www.artistshannonrankin.com
PG. 194-195

JOSHUA SPENCER
Los Angeles, CA, USA
www.joshuaspencerphoto.com
PG. VIII, 198-199 (PHOTOGRAPHY)

VICTORIA ARONSON
Los Angeles, CA, USA
PG. VIII, 198-199 (HAIR/MAKEUP)

SHOUT OUTS

Thank you to our agent, Erin Malone, at WME2 for kicking ass and taking names. And thank you to Brenda Copeland, Kate Griffin, and the entire Hyperion team for believing in the mission of SoulPancake and bringing this book to life.

Our sincere gratitude goes out to the brilliant minds who contributed their valuable time to help kick off the conversation—Amy Sedaris, David Lynch, Dr. Drew, Harold Ramis, Heather Armstrong, Jesse Dylan, Justin Vernon, and Saul Williams. And especially to Josh Ritter, who wrote and recorded a song just for SoulPancake.

To all of the artists whose work is featured on these pages: Your creativity blows us away. Thank you for joining us on this adventure. In particular, thank you to Chahn Chung, Kapono Chung, and Albert Ignacio, the three ingenious designers who powered through long nights and endured our OCD to turn each page into a visual masterpiece.

A big thanks to our extended SoulPancake squad—including the bold and dedicated members of the SP Brain Lab and the innovative gurus on the technology team—who keep the SoulPancake web community happy and well fed.

And finally to our families and friends, who put up with our 2 a.m., sleep-interrupting conference calls; trekked across the badlands to get contracts signed; and helped us "purple it"—you are a continuous source of love, comfort, laughter, opinions, ideas, coffee, feta cheese, lemon almonds, spare rooms, and bumpy futons. We don't have space to name you all, but please know that we adore and thank each and every one of you. Especially Astrid Alauda. (Google it.)

Oh, wait. One more: Thank you, technology gods, for giving us Skype, Google Docs, and iPhones, without which this nomadic, cross-country (and sometimes cross-continental) crew would never have been able to write this book. Amen. SP out. Nap time. ∎

205